True to Experience

True to Experience

H. A. Williams C.R.

Edited by Eileen Mable

CONTINUUM
London and New York

I resolved that I would not preach about any aspect of Christian belief unless it had become part of my own life-blood. . . . All I could speak of were those things which I had proved true in my own experience by living them and thus knowing them at first hand.
The True Wilderness

Continuum

Wellington House, 125 Strand, London WC2R 0BB

370 Lexington Avenue, New York, NY 10017–6503

First Published 1984

This edition published 2000 by Continuum

British Library Cataloguing-in-Publication Data

A catalogue record for this book is available from the British Library.

ISBN 0-8264-4924-5

Typeset by T&O Graphics, Oulton Broad

Printed and bound in Great Britain by Biddles Ltd,

Guildford and King's Lynn

Contents

Acknowledgements

The editor and publishers are grateful to those listed below for their kind permission to reprint the following extracts: Andre Deutsch for the quotation from *Not Waving but Drowning* (1952) by Stevie Smith (p. 7); Faber and Faber Ltd for the quotation from *Four Quartets* (1944) by T. S. Eliot, published by Harcourt Brace Jovanovich Inc in USA (1943), (p. 231); Cambridge University Press for extracts from *Soundings* (1962), edited by A. R. Vidler; A. R. Mowbray and Co. Ltd for extracts from *God's Wisdom in Christ's Cross* (1960) by H. A. Williams, and *The Four Last Things* (1960) by H. A. Williams; *The Times* for the extract from 'What Freud and Jung mean for religion' (20 June 1970); Constable and Co. Ltd for extracts from *The True Wilderness* (1965) by H. A. Williams, and *Objections to Christian Belief* (1963) by H. A. Williams; Darton, Longman and Todd for extracts from *Becoming What I Am* (1977) by H. A. Williams, published by the Fortress Press in USA under the title *The Simplicity of Power* (1977); BBC Radio 4 for extracts from 'Conflict and victory' (16 April 1976).

Editor's Preface

My aim in this Anthology is to make the major themes of Harry Williams's thinking clearly and easily available. Those themes have indeed dictated the framework of this book. But, because everything Harry Williams has written is so deeply rooted in our experience of life — life which is defiantly and exuberantly untidy and which resists all our efforts to contain it within neat categories — the divisions of this Anthology are not as definitive as I originally intended them to be.

There is a natural progression in the book; and the reader will certainly find within any section the theme indicated by its title. But he will also find much else. The great themes of death and resurrection and of the need for self-acceptance, for example, cannot be confined within the sections allotted to them; they recur frequently and sometimes unexpectedly throughout the book. In a few instances, where passages particularly relevant to a section have had to be included elsewhere, I have provided cross-references but I have not done so generally.

The majority of Harry Williams's books comprise sermons, addresses and talks originally given to particular audiences. A number of pieces in this Anthology therefore contain topical references. These are usually self-explanatory but I have on a few occasions added a footnote.

True Resurrection stands apart. It was written directly as a book and, as Harry Williams's most detailed exploration of the experience of resurrection, it contains long passages of sustained argument, sections of which cannot satisfactorily be lifted out of context. I have included passages from *True Resurrection* here; but the book is very much a unity and only a complete reading does it full justice.

The making of an anthology necessarily involves difficult decisions and it is inevitable that some readers already acquainted with Harry Williams's work will regret the omission of one or more favourite passages. Personal preference, as well as the need to provide as representative a selection as possible, has, of course, influenced me. There is, however, a further criterion. Without wishing to claim that this Anthology is totally definitive of Harry Williams's current thinking, I have tried not to include anything that would contradict or be inconsistent with it. This means that I have, albeit regretfully, included very little from *Jesus and the Resurrection* (1951) and nothing at all from the eloquent sermons that have survived from his time as a curate at All Saints', Margaret Street.

There is a break, although not a complete discontinuity, between this early work, produced before Harry Williams's breakdown, and his later books. The former certainly contains hints of themes which came to their full flowering in the books written after psycho-analysis had freed Harry Williams to write directly from experience and vividly to relate that experience to the Christian gospel in terms that make sense to many for whom traditional religious language has little meaning. But to have included in this Anthology passages which, however interesting in the development of Harry Williams's thought, no longer represent his understanding, would have been inappropriate and misleading.

I am grateful for the help I have received in compiling this Anthology, particularly from the Right Rev. Stanley Booth-Clibborn, formerly Vicar of Great St Mary's Church, Cambridge, from Dr Glen Cavaliero, Canon Eric

James and the late Rev. David Sparrow. I also acknowledge the assistance of the staff of the various libraries
consulted by myself and the publishers.

My husband, Norman, who died before publication of
this book, gave me generously and unstintingly of his time
and understanding during the months of preparation, as
also did Miss Ida Stretton: to both of them I am most
deeply indebted.

Finally, I wish to express my gratitude to Harry Williams
himself for his trust and encouragement, for his ready help
when I have needed it and, above all, for all that I have
learned from him over the years. This last is a debt which I
gladly acknowledge but cannot hope to repay.

Eileen Mable

May 1983

Introduction by the Dean of St Paul's

Father Harry Williams is one of the very few preachers who draws a congregation today simply because he is preaching. His printed sermons enjoy a wide circulation. Those concerned to discover what contemporary Christianity has to offer in a serious search for meaning in life turn to *The True Wilderness* as a revelation of the riches found within the Christian tradition. Harry Williams has a deep concern for the Jesus Christ unveiled in the Scriptures, the Prayer Book and the Christian classics and, building on those foundations, his assertion that "only the truth you discover for yourself has the power of truth for you" is exceptionally compelling.

In editing this collection of his writings, Eileen Mable has performed a double service, both to those who have heard Father Williams's sermons or who have read his books over several decades and will be happy to possess this distillation and also to those who come to the author for the first time, and who will be drawn back to the published sources. His autobiography, *Some Day I'll Find You*, is a rare triumph, witty and entertaining and yet taking us to the depths of faith and prayer, and now we are given an anthology to set beside it.

Preaching at the Three Hours' Devotion in St Paul's in 1982, Harry Williams led his congregation from seven words from the Cross, the traditional material for Christian meditation, to the struggles of living the faith today despite the sense of guilt, compromise and self-

analysis natural amongst a twentieth-century congregation. There was nothing smooth and no pious patter of
platitudes. Instead, as someone said afterwards, one
understood oneself and the gospel story with a fundamental simplicity which was refreshing and challenging.
Harry Williams has always honestly faced the objections to
Christian belief and, in consequence, wins our trust in his
very positive teaching. His God is alive and alert, the spirit
in the heart of our personality.

Especially in days when so many conduct their religious search in the reflective quiet of their own homes and
not at the public worship of the various churches, this
Anthology will fulfil a felt need. Some will find the extracts
on Incarnation, Wilderness, Cross and Resurrection ideal
for an hour by themselves at Christmas or Lent, Holy
Week or Easter. Others who wonder whether the religious
institutions can really match the demands of today will
find here an invitation to explore the Catholic faith.
Others, again, will be among those many thousands who
have experienced the sense of a personal companion in
their pilgrimage when listening to sermons of Father Harry
Williams or hearing him on radio or TV. I believe that all
readers of this Anthology will be grateful for someone who
has not shirked the risks of re-thinking and experiencing
the central core of Christian faith and being prepared to
state his conclusions openly and honestly, and often with
rare grace and a happy twist of humour.

Alan Webster

Foreword

James Mitchell suggested to me some time ago that he would like to publish an Anthology of my work. I greeted the suggestion with very considerable reserve, as I did not think my writings anything like weighty enough for such treatment. I still think they may well not be. But since publishing my autobiography *Some Day I'll Find You*, I have received a considerable number of letters from complete strangers asking for my views on this or that aspect of Christian faith and life. Answering these with whatever adequacy I am capable of has been more or less a year's work. And this has made me wonder whether an Anthology might not after all be useful.

I am deeply grateful to Eileen Mable for the patience, sensitivity and utter selflessness, not to mention the hard work, that she has devoted to the task of compiling this Anthology. She has given to it a skill and devotion much greater than the material deserves. And I have more than a suspicion that she has made it look better than it is.

H. A. Williams

1
Beginnings

Openness

An invisible as well as a visible world — openness to
life — openness to mystery in all things — never be
content with half a loaf — a question of motive — the
terrible risk of absolute love — the journey from the
city within to the city of God — guided into all
truth — our darkness, the beginning of God's light.

I happen to have been born in England of Christian parents, and, with the best will in the world, I cannot be somebody else. So, inevitably, it is with Christianity that I have been most concerned. It is Christianity that I have loved and hated. It is Christianity that I have believed and disbelieved and believed again in a different way. It is with Christianity that I have wrestled, trying to force from it the secret which lies beneath all the pretentious nonsense, the love which lies beneath all the cruelty and the fear. It is Christianity that I have interpreted, discarded, reinterpreted, discarded, and reinterpreted again. Certainly I would have a different story to tell had I been born in India of Hindu parents. But I wasn't. After all, historical accident is always at the centre of our lives. Last vac you married Betty who is at Girton. But suppose you had gone to Oxford? . . .

Why, then, am I a Christian?

Fundamentally, I think, because it is impossible for me to believe that there is no more to reality than the things which can be seen and heard, weighed and measured, things which can be subjected to statistical analysis. I am a Christian because my experience has forced me to believe that there is an invisible world as well as the visible one, that however real may be all that is physical, animal and material, I cannot begin to make sense of my experience simply in those terms alone. I cannot escape from what could be described as the spiritual dimension of life. Now that, I know, sounds grandiose, but what in fact I mean is very ordinary. Let me give you one or two examples.

Over the past few years I have got to know Fred very well. Like everybody else he has his good and bad points, not to mention his eccentricities. I am only too aware, especially when I am annoyed with him, that there is a great deal about him which can be explained in scientific terms. He is clever, but then his father is a professor and he went to a school noted for the academic ability of its staff. He is moody, but then his mother is a manic-depressive. He can be lazy, but then a recent blood-test showed him to have a calcium deficiency. He is always at ease in company, but then his grandfather was a peer. In other words, genetics, physics, biochemistry, psychology and sociology can tell me a lot about Fred. They provide me with a valid description of him as far as they go, and they can go quite far when I want to explain him away. But, for all their validity and my irritation, the real Fred somehow eludes these scientific descriptions.

I have to admit that he is much more than the sum-total of these respective analyses. He belongs to the world of scientific enquiry all right – at times he seems to belong to it with a vengeance – but he also belongs to a world where information about him has become irrelevant because I have established communion with him. We had dinner together last night and talked until the early hours, and I never once thought of him genetically or bio-chemically or psychologically or sociologically. He was just him, and I enjoyed his company enormously. It made me realize that, although the Fred about whom I can be scientifically informed is real enough, he is far less real than the Fred I dined with, the Fred with whom I was in personal communion.

Perhaps I could put it this way – I am very fond of Fred, but the Fred I am fond of is not a collection of scientific information. He is more real to me than a statistical table. Indeed he is far too real for anything like adequate intellectual description at all. Yet I can know him, know him intimately, but here knowing means being in communion with him. If I were a poet I might be able to throw out hints, think up one or two images, which might suggest to you what the quintessential Fred is like. If I were a painter, I might be able, in a portrait of him, to let you see a little of the mysterious reality which lies behind his physical appearance.

Here, then, in Fred I am confronted with an invisible world, a spiritual dimension, and the invisible is not less real but more real than the visible, the spiritual not less real but more real than the material. Statistical tables are doubtless interesting and informative, but you can't be fond of them, you can't have dinner and laugh with them.

However, don't let's get fixated on Fred, even if his father is a professor and his grandfather a peer. We must look for other examples of the invisible world or spiritual dimension. What about music — let's say a Beethoven symphony?

From one point of view music is as rational as mathematics, and therefore the symphony can be analysed rationally with almost mathematical precision. The musical idioms Beethoven uses can be described and related to the idioms used by his predecessors and successors. Up to a point the symphony is capable of intellectual description, and the description is perfectly valid. But in the end the symphony calls not for description but for surrender. If we are to know it fully we must do more than study it. We must give ourselves up to it, and what we give ourselves up to is not just a pattern of sounds arranged in certain mathematical sequences. It is a realm of wonder, love and praise, made accessible to us by the sounds we hear, but infinitely more than the actual sum of those sounds themselves. You will remember E. M. Forster's description in *Howards End*:

"Beethoven brought back the gusts of splendour, the heroism, the youth, the magnificence of life and death, and amid vast roarings of a superhuman joy, he led his Fifth Symphony to its conclusion."

You would have to be a very dull dog, a musical pedant of the most boring kind, if all you heard in a symphony was what was literally audible. Or to say the same thing with a different use of words — heard melodies are sweet, but those unheard are sweeter. And the heard melodies become most meaningful when they open our ears to the unheard.

Alternatively, what about something which is deeply and uproariously funny? Our uncontrollable laughter exceeds any rational reaction the occasion of the joke could have produced. We feel liberated by what is funny. Why? Because the funny event and our laughter at it means that we have caught a whiff of something that isn't part of the grey, cold world of measurement and logical sequence. As we laugh we are indeed still in bondage to that world of hard necessity, the world of the multiplication table, yet as we laugh we also rise above that world because we twig that we belong to another world as well, a world which cuts this world down to size and in which we are free to be ourselves unhindered by what cabins and confines us in the visible, tangible order. All genuine laughter, when it is free from malice or bitterness, bears its unconscious witness to the invisible world, the spiritual dimension. (That, I suspect, is why there is so much laughter in monasteries.) What makes us laugh is the sheer contrast, the sheer incongruity, between the spiritual dimension where we most deeply belong, and the slings and arrows which impale us and the limitations which confine us in the empirical, observable world.

I am a Christian, then, because I cannot make sense of my experience simply in terms of what is material and capable of scientific investigation and statistical analysis. As in Fred, the Beethoven symphony and the funny joke, so in all life, I am inescapably aware of the presence of the unseen.

If God so made us that only he himself can ultimately satisfy us, he does not withhold that gift of himself. It is ours already, but, being too blind to recognize it, we have to discover it, not in religious theory, but in the warmth and sweetness and dryness and terror of actual living.

One thing is necessary.
Luke 10:42

What did Jesus mean by "the one thing necessary"? He didn't mean a creed, or a morality, or a programme of action, not even an ideal. Still less was he trying to sell salvation machinery — "be converted or be baptized or always let your conscience be your guide". He was pointing out that people, even people with the best will in the world, tend to live poverty-stricken and frustrated lives because they are content to remain on the superficial surface of themselves, and so of the world, and don't see the necessity of going deeper into life. Because this keeps them shallow people, they mistake appearances for reality. And when you mistake appearances for reality, life becomes stale and unprofitable. It can imprison and persecute you, and you can make the most hideous mistakes about everybody and everything.

Do you remember Stevie Smith's poem about the man who died drowning while his friends were watching him? They thought he was having fun,

> *But still he lay moaning:*
> *I was much further out*
> *than you thought*
> *And not waving but drowning.*

"Poor chap," his friends said afterwards, "he always loved larking". But

> *(Still the dead one lay moaning)*
> *I was much too far out all my life*
> *And not waving but drowning.*

If we are shallow people, our estimates of others and their behaviour will be superficial, and this is perhaps the most refined form of cruelty possible – a cruelty hidden from us as we think the drowning man is simply conceited, or bad-tempered, or rude, or just trying to be funny, while in fact he is a man in desperate trouble signalling for help. That is the kind of misjudgement we make when we live only on the surface of what we are. . . .

But the worst effect of living shallowly, of mistaking appearances for reality, is that it turns everything into a dead end, leaving us feeling "So what?" We fail to see that things point beyond themselves to what is deeper and greater, and that it is only when they thus point beyond themselves that they are truly themselves. If in a birthday cake you see only sugar, flour, butter and egg, then it isn't

truly a birthday cake. It is a birthday cake only in so far as it
points beyond itself to the celebration it has been made to
mark. Sugar, flour, butter, egg – our danger in this
scientific age is that of reducing everything to its constituent
parts so that the world becomes no more than a heap of
dismantled machinery. It is the danger of failing to see *what*
things are, the values and realities they embody and point to
(thus becoming fully themselves) – of failing to see *what*
things are because we are so occupied with analysing and
dissecting them. In this age of space travel we need to be
reminded of a warning given by D. H. Lawrence.

> The universe is dead for us, and how
> is it to come alive again?
> "Knowledge" has killed the sun,
> making it a ball of gas with spots;
> "knowledge" has killed the moon – it
> is a dead little earth fretted with
> extinct craters as with smallpox.

Thus, as Lawrence saw, there are whole areas of
beauty and grace and wonder and mystery which remain
closed against us. Our life is basically impoverished. We live
in a small dungeon cell, hitting our head against its wall. We
cannot lift up our eyes unto the hills from whence cometh
our help because we are too busy and preoccupied to notice
them, and in any case what are they but so much material
for intellectual analysis of one kind or another?

Jesus saw that life on these terms is just not on. He saw
that it makes life intolerable in the most literal sense. It
forces us to live in a wasteland which combines the horror
of infinite emptiness with the horror of extreme claustro-
phobic confinement. It dehumanizes us by robbing us of

communion with our world. We contact everything only in its disrupted externality (which is no human contact at all) and, in consequence, we ourselves feel not like people but things. None of us, please God, has yet walked to the end of that road. Few of us so far have probably gone very far along it, for our humanity is too resilient to be easily destroyed. But all of us must have travelled a mile or two of it, and some of us considerably further. It is vitally important that we should know what we are doing, that we should know the degree in which we are evading the one thing necessary.

But what then is this one necessary thing? It is difficult to describe what is so comprehensive and fundamental. For any one particular description is liable, on its own, to give a wrong impression. So I must ask you to take into account that whatever I say is only one way of putting it among endless other ways.

The one thing necessary is to be open and prepared for mystery. It is to understand that familiar things are not just or only familiar things, but that they invite us on a voyage of discovery in order to show us a richness, a subtlety, a depth, which formerly we never dreamt they possessed. The one thing necessary is to be at least on the look out for that to happen. It is to be expectant as we live in our ordinary world, because that world is not really ordinary at all in the usual sense, but it is full of hitherto unperceived and un-imagined wonder. For our world, like all worlds, is the dwelling-place of mystery. But mystery, remember, is not the same thing as mystification. Mystery is not to be abstruse or tortuous or underhand in our thinking. Nor is mystery a riddle or enigma which in principle can be solved, and which in time will be solved, by intellectual effort.

Mystery is the atmosphere in which we live (if only our

eyes are open to see it). It glimmers and twinkles all around us and beckons us to communion with itself. And the communion is a *felt* communion, not something we can intellectually dissect or analyse. Mystery often impinges on us as a Presence, an inexhaustible Presence everywhere in all things. To be aware of the Presence, to be aware of the mystery in all things is not to find that those things have faded away or been melted down. On the contrary, to perceive the mystery in anything is to find it more itself than we ever found it before. For it is in pointing beyond themselves that things are most themselves (like the birthday cake), and it is thus that we discover their full and real identity. That is one of the ways in which perceiving mystery makes life infinitely rich and satisfying. For it is appearances which suck us dry and deaden us, not reality. . . .

How are we to be open and prepared for mystery? How are we to make the one thing necessary our own? How are we to be fully persons? It is pretty certain that we shan't be able to do it without periods of quiet, without reflection, without times when of set purpose we sit still and wait — wait expectantly. And we have to learn how to sit still and wait, and to learn we shall almost certainly need a teacher. What I am speaking of is sometimes called contemplation, and we need to discover from books and people and our own experience how we can contemplate most fruitfully. It isn't an immediately exciting trip. You can't contemplate for kicks. It requires discipline and patience like anything worthwhile, the willingness to put up with long spells when nothing seems to be happening. Yes, we shall need advice, and we shall certainly need common sense.

For in the end we shall have to discover our own particular way of proceeding, for ultimately each person's way is unique to himself. There is no general recipe or formula. There is no standard way of sitting still and waiting expectantly for life to reveal to you the depth and richness of its mystery. And when that revelation comes, it generally comes unexpectedly, when we've ceased really to think anything will happen. And the revelation comes as pure gift, not as something we have earned but something freely given to us, something homely as well as wonderful, something which we then realize we have known somewhere in our bones all the time.

This exercise of waiting expectantly is, incidentally, what Christians call prayer, just as the mystery revealed all around us is what Christians call God. But I am not trying to convert you. I am merely pointing out how intolerable it is to live on the superficial surface of things and how life can be satisfying only if we live deeply. It is intolerable not to be human, not to be a person, and to be human, to be a person, we have got to find depth. And to find depth we have got to wait expectantly in stillness; we have got to pray. It is the one thing necessary.

The kingdom of heaven is like unto a
merchant man, seeking goodly pearls:
who, when he had found one pearl of
great price, went and sold all that he
had, and bought it.
Matthew 13:45

The merchant did not find the one pearl of great price at the beginning of his career. He must have been in business some time before he eventually discovered it. For, in the first place, he had to accumulate the capital needed to buy it. Had it come his way at the start he would not have had enough goods to sell to realize the fortune required for its purchase. And, secondly, without much experience he might not have been able to recognize its supreme value. The instant understanding of its worth could come only after a long time spent in sorting, comparing and evaluating. Had the merchant refused to trade in lesser pearls, he would never have acquired the one pearl of great price.

Jesus said that the kingdom of heaven was like this merchant man. At the very least this means that the kingdom is not something which can be immediately presented to you on a plate, so that all you have to do is to put it into your pocket and feel good. You will find many devout Christians who have forgotten what Jesus said and who will present the kingdom of heaven to you in exactly this way. It means, they will tell you, adhesion to a given form of doctrinal orthodoxy. Believe this, that and the other, and there, you've got the kingdom. But you haven't got it. All you've got is an excuse to stop looking for it. You may commend the views you have thus accepted with passionate earnestness and zeal, but these may only show that deep down you are afraid that you have been fobbed off with an artificial pearl. All fanaticism is a strategy to prevent doubt from becoming conscious. And meanwhile the apparent agnostic infidel in the rooms above may in his own manner still be seeking for the kingdom of heaven, while you aren't.

Or, some people will tell you that the kingdom consists in obedience to a traditional system of ethics. Do this and don't do that, and yours is the kingdom. Obedience of this kind often looks like a virtue. In fact, it is always a blasphemy. A blasphemy against oneself. To base and regulate one's life upon other people's rules – even when they call them God's Law – this is blasphemous because it is to choose slavery when you could be free. Freedom involves the discovery by each of us of the law of his own being: how he, as a unique person, can express sincerely and fearlessly what he is. And this discovery can be made only by the courageous acceptance of experience, through suffering and joy, through disillusion and fulfilment. If you are content to be conventional or conventionally unconventional, if you are content to be like somebody else and accept as your own the rules of a given type of person, then you have abandoned looking for the kingdom of heaven.

Or, others will tell you that the kingdom consists in stimulating within yourself a certain type of religious experience which is miscalled conversion. If, they say, you haven't had this particular sort of religious experience, then you are outside the kingdom. The trouble is that when you examine the required experience carefully and deeply, you find that it isn't essentially religious at all. True, in the case we are considering, the required feelings are evoked by symbols long associated with religion. But precisely similar feelings can be evoked by symbols which have no religious associations at all. Think of the comforting warmth, the escape from isolation, the wonderful sense of purpose and mission, evoked in Germany by Adolf Hitler. To the half-blind, like ourselves, it is not always so easy as it seems to distinguish between the kingdom of heaven and the kingdom of hell.

But how then are we to enter into the kingdom of heaven? How can we find the one pearl of great price?

Only thus: by refusing to be satisfied with anything less than what is totally satisfying. I don't mean what *should* satisfy us, but what in fact *does*. You know how all invitations are kind invitations and how at all parties we

enjoyed ourselves immensely. That is just a polite convention. We mustn't treat any prescription for life with a sort
of pious *politesse* trying to persuade ourselves that it satisfies when it doesn't. Of course, there is the old saying that
half a loaf is better than no bread – a wise maxim in a
number of circumstances. But as a policy for living it is
utterly irreligious and, if we follow it, it will exclude us
absolutely from the kingdom of heaven. For, without
deadening part of us, without doing injury to what God has
made, we can never be content with half a loaf. We can
never be content with less than total satisfaction.

Consider, for instance, the God you have been
brought up with and sometimes worship and vaguely serve
and perhaps half disbelieve. To be honest, isn't this God
rather like half a loaf? Wouldn't it be true to say that he
satisfies you only in part? If so, you must spend your time
here looking for a better God – you can look for a better
God by reading, by thinking, by discussion, by the experience of common worship and private prayer, by living,
knocking about and being knocked about. You won't go
down from here with a whole loaf. But you may go down
with the inner certainty that in the end you will get the
whole. And that's the meaning of faith: it is basing your life
on the conviction that to those who ask it shall be given,
that those who seek shall find, that to those who knock it
shall be opened, however long we have to ask and seek and
knock.

Or take our way of life, what we live for, what we aim
at doing, what we value most. Does that satisfy us? Or does
it leave a void somewhere? I'm afraid that's the sort of thing
we simply can't take on trust. We've got to find it out for
ourselves. Some things seem to satisfy us fully for a time,
and then we gradually discover that they fail to cater for a

quite important part of us. There are times, for instance, when some of us imagine that we can live simply by every word which proceedeth out of the mouth of God. And then we learn that we can't, that we have also to live by bread. The warm human nature we are tempted to despise because we share it with all sinners refuses to be ignored. Or, on the other hand, we may imagine that we can live by bread alone, that worldly success and gratified instincts are all we need to satisfy us fully. The bread may remain new for a time, then it gets stale and suddenly we realize that it has been turned into a stone. We look around and find ourselves in a wasteland surrounded by heaps of rusty abandoned junk. But don't take this from me or anybody else. For if you don't discover it for yourself, in your heart of hearts you will always envy the people you call worldly or wicked. And envy excludes satisfaction.

And this brings us back to the merchant. We said he had to accumulate the capital he needed to buy the pearl of great price. And it was real solid wealth. We often think we can buy the one pearl with paper money. We are sincere enough when we add up our paper pounds. We don't want or intend to deceive ourselves. But it is very easy for us to forget that there is precious little real wealth behind the notes we are counting.

Our intentions and acts of will are the paper money. We resolve to do this, to be that, to give ourselves to the other. We forget that there are large areas of the self where the writ of the will simply doesn't run. I resolve, shall we say, to be loving to everybody. That resolve of mine is the paper pound I pay for the pearl of great price. I forget that my capacity to love is as yet stunted and immature, and that, in the absence of such real wealth, my resolve is worth very little. And so I expect to obtain the pearl and wonder why I don't. I expect to feel fulfilled and satisfied and all I feel is tired and on edge.

What we have to learn is that our real capital accumulates slowly, and often without our noticing it. The earth, as Jesus said, beareth fruit of itself. Theologians would say that we grow as people only through the grace of God. But grace isn't a sort of spiritual petrol. It is the creative quality of life itself — all the things we do, all the things that happen to us, working, arguing, listening, playing, falling in love, all the splendours and the miseries, all the pleasure and the pain — it is thus that our real capital slowly accumulates until in the end we can honour the paper pound of our resolves with the golden sovereign of our whole selves.

And what about recognizing the pearl of great price? What about the instant understanding of its worth?

Christianity presents us with a man upon a cross, a man whose teaching still has the power to thrill, whatever we believe about him, a man who gave everything away in love for others, even life itself. And it points to this man in his death-agony and says that there, in utter complete self-giving, there alone is what satisfies totally. Most of us have brief moments when we know with absolute certainty that so to give ourselves away in love is the full, perfect satisfaction for which we crave. But such moments do not stay. The Crucified soon passes as in a cloud out of our sight. And we are left only half-believing, left to win the truth for ourselves, by trial and error, by false hopes and shattered illusions, and by joy unspeakable and full of glory.

There is nothing in this world or the next, absolutely nothing, which cannot, and will not, be turned into the valid currency we need to buy the one pearl of great price. That is what is meant when we say that we are redeemed.

If you want to discover the difference which Jesus made to mankind, and go to the New Testament to find out, the answer given is the casting out of people's lives of fear. Fear, in the New Testament, is considered to be the root of all evil. It is fear which makes men selfish, it is fear which makes them hate, it is fear which makes them blind, it is fear which makes them mad. Fear casts out love, as love casts out fear. Which of the two therefore am I going to choose?

It may well be that in this matter I am a house divided against itself. For instance, yesterday I behaved unselfishly. I stood down in the interests of somebody else. But this hasn't brought me any happiness or peace. My unselfishness wasn't recognized, and I feel angry, miserable, and on edge. Why? Because I was unselfish through fear – fear of being thought selfish and thus losing other people's good opinion. And, probably, mixed up with this, a more subtle and less identifiable fear that somehow things would go wrong with me if I had acted selfishly. No wonder, therefore, that I feel all prickles with regard to the other chap who doesn't share my inhibitions, isn't at all afraid of being selfish, and has thus, at my expense, pushed himself to the centre of the stage without caring a damn. How can I help envying him like hell? You remember the woman in Belloc's rhyme:

> *Though unbelieving as a beast,*
> *She didn't worry in the least,*
> *But drank as hard as she was able,*
> *And sang and danced upon the table.*

And she makes poor frightened little me feel very wretched with envy. For I have tried to be good by means of an evil thing: fear.

But suppose I have behaved unselfishly out of love? Suppose I knew with deep certainty that I could only be my full self by giving, and that this is what love means. Then yesterday, when I acted unselfishly, I should not have been denying myself, not in the least. On the contrary, I should have been affirming myself. I should have been mobilizing all I am in order to be fully me. And today I should feel happy and at peace, because I should not be a house divided against itself. The self-assertive go-getter for whom I stood down could not in the least exploit my unselfishness. Nobody on earth could. For it would simply have been me being myself. And that would be the end of it. This is the omnipotent strength which comes from a house not divided against itself.

Now, I don't think for one moment that I can summon up this strength by simple willpower. The very idea of will-power implies division – two things pushing each other in opposite directions. What I need I must be given, and that is more light, deeper perception, a less clouded vision of what life is about. How am I to get it? Only in the ancient school of experience, by trial and error, by pain and joy, and, most of all, by faith, a confidence that, in spite of all appearances to the contrary, life is on my side and not against me. This is the confidence which Jesus brought to men. It was summed up by St Paul in ten words, "If God be for us, who can be against us?" When I begin to be convinced of that fact, I shall begin to be a house not divided against itself.

We are somewhere very frightened of love without recognizing at all clearly that we are. For absolute love, God's love, makes us fully ourselves, instead of the half people we generally are. And to become fully yourself is a terrible risk. It would commit you to God knows what and lead you God knows where. If I open my heart in simplicity to God's love I might soon find myself in Bangladesh or something of that sort, or I might find myself disagreeing or even agreeing with Mrs Whitehouse. Or letting in God's love might prompt me to join the Campaign for Homosexual Equality, or the Tory Party, or it might lead me actively to support the Tribune Group; it might make me concerned about the oppressed peoples of the Third World or even about my neighbour next door who is lonely. And God's love has been known to make the most respectable people enjoy a pub crawl. And letting in God's love is no guarantee at all that I will necessarily remain an enthusiastic member of the Church of England or even of the Anglo-Catholic set-up. And so, not so much in our minds consciously as in our bones unconsciously, we see to it that when we pray we keep ourselves tied up in knots. It is much safer. Let us keep on the armour of our sophistication and plump for security.

But then of course we miss the glorious liberty of the children of God. We remain half dead, too afraid to know what life is. And missing out on the splendour and warm intimacy of God's love, we become hooked on some compensatory activity like overwork or keeping up with the Jones's, or drink, or sex, or it might even be religiosity and church going. Such compensatory activities don't in practice compensate at all.

Society – the city, the home, the school, the college, the university, however we divide it up – society is not only an external reality, something outside us over there. Society is also inside us and part of what we are. We have been fashioned and moulded by it. A child often inherits some of the physical features of its parents. "Ah," says the friend of the family, "you've got your mother's eyes." In the same way we inherit or absorb a great deal of the mental outlook and emotional attitudes of the society into which we are born. We look at things through eyes, partly at least, already conditioned for us. We see and feel things in ways partly pre-determined. This is society inside us. And it is by means of this society inside us that we feel we belong. It is by means of this common stamp that we are aware of our membership one to another. We don't feel isolated because we share much of our inner thoughts and feelings with those around us. The external city to which we belong is built in miniature within the individual heart and mind.

A curious and sometimes amusing consequence follows. The society outside us to which we belong may be extremely tolerant. Cambridge is, for instance. At the same time, the society inside us may be intolerant to an extreme degree. That is the sort of situation which makes a man into a rebel without a cause. His life is one long protest against apparently nothing – since there is nothing in the external order he wishes to change. What he is up against, without knowing it, is the intolerant tyrant inside. I remember, a year or two ago, having a television discussion with a very militant agnostic lady. Throughout I was at pains to emphasize what happened to be the case – that I was very much in the dark and certain about nothing. However, at the end, the good lady looked at me severely and said, "You people might sometimes admit you don't know everything."

Clearly she was not addressing the actual clergyman sitting opposite her in the studio. She was addressing a built-in clergyman which was a part of herself.

But towards this built-in city or society we are by no means necessarily hostile. Far from it. More often we regard this internal realm with enormous respect which sometimes merges into worship. And even if we are hostile, our very hostility is a sign that another part of us cherishes and values what we must therefore all the more emphatically condemn. (That is why tirades against sin generally reveal what the speaker most fancies.) Yes, the city inside us is an object of compelling awe. How could it be otherwise? That city was built because we had to belong to a world. In our earliest days we shouldn't have survived at all unless we belonged to a world which would feed and look after us. And since man is by nature social, we still need a society to belong to.

No wonder, therefore, that the city outside makes such a deep and lasting mark within us. No wonder we feel we must guard this internal citadel. No wonder we endue it with the value of life itself. No wonder that, for its better protection, we often identify the city inside with truth and goodness. If we want to be polite we call it our inherited convictions; if we want to be rude we call it our inherited prejudices; if we want to be eloquent we call it the great tradition we have been born to serve; if we want to be religious we call it the will of God. But no matter what we call this society within us, and however much from time to time we may want to kick this or that aspect of it, fundamentally we feel with fear and with passion that its preservation is a matter of life and death.

"Whoever seeks to save his life", said Jesus, "will lose it; and whoever loses it will save it, and live." You have come to the university not first of all to equip yourself

technically for a job. You have come here first of all to lose
your life and save it and live. If this place does for you what it
should, you will knock up against all sorts of people with
different views about the most fundamental things. You will
think and talk and argue and laugh. You will enjoy yourself,
but you will also sometimes suffer. For in the general atmosphere of thought and discussion and criticism and laughter,
the city inside you may well be invaded and overthrown.
What you have so far considered obviously true or false may
now seem not so obvious. What so far has appeared as
certainly good or bad may now seem not so certain.

   If by temperament you are an establishment man, certain features of the establishment may begin to look shabby
or dishonest. If by temperament you are an anti-
establishment man, certain features of your rebellion may
begin to look childish and silly. All in all, you will be
releasing your grip upon what so far you have lived by, in
order that it may be weighed in the balance and its real
worth discovered. This invasion and exposure of the city
within is, from one point of view, exciting. But it is also
painfully disconcerting since it leaves us for the time being
without a world. We find ourselves strangers walking along
an unknown path, instead of respected inhabitants of a
familiar town. It feels as if we don't belong anywhere, and
we are therefore not unlike the first Christian converts
losing the warm life of their Jewish or pagan past.

   And now, as then, the cost of this renunciation is too
great for many people. They seek to save their life by the
blind acceptance of an official orthodoxy – not because
after examination and trial they have found the orthodoxy
true but because it gives them immediate protection, like a
mother's arms, and saves them from the danger of standing
on their own feet. But by thus seeking to save their life they

really lose it. They stagnate spiritually, shut up tight against the questions life poses and the demands it makes, making the observances of their particular orthodoxy into a substitute for living. Inevitably they become intolerant, telling us that at all costs we must believe what they say because it is really God speaking. Fundamentally they are frightened people, and what they are afraid of is the life which destroys before it animates.

But what of those others who are willing to lose their life and live? Those who are brave enough to have their cosy but confined city destroyed in order to find another which is without limit in the grandeur of its majesty? At times they will find themselves in the desert. At other times they will find themselves in pastures more green than they have ever known before. They will be looking for a city which hath foundations whose builder and maker is God. Their journey to the City of God may bring them to worship in this chapel or it may lead them away from it. But in either case, whether they are present here or absent, what they are doing will be shown forth and lived through Sunday by Sunday. For on every Sunday morning in this place bread is broken and wine poured out in remembrance of one who did not seek to save his life, but lost it and is alive for evermore. He is mankind, and his cross and his glory belong to us. As by unfamiliar paths we journey to the unknown and find ourselves renewed by that bracing atmosphere, with him we shall be dying and rising from the dead.

When he, the Spirit of truth, is come,
he will guide you into all truth.
St John 16:13

Nowhere in the New Testament do we find words more terrifying than these. Perhaps you think it strange that they should be called that. Obviously some people fear the truth – bigots, reactionaries, obscurantists of one sort or another – but not us with our liberal education and open minds. If Cambridge has done for us what it's meant to do, then surely we, of all people, can welcome with serenity and pleasure our Saviour's promise that his Spirit will guide us into all the truth.

There are, however, two kinds of truth which I'm going to call the outside kind and the inside. Universities are concerned only with the outside kind of truth. They train us to observe objects or ideas as accurately as possible and to see as fully as possible how these objects or ideas are related to each other. From us, as people, what we study keeps its distance. It's a sort of mental money – worrying only if you haven't got any; otherwise our property, over which we have complete control. So we speak of the expert as somebody who has mastered the subject. And where there is mastery, there is no sense of risk or feeling of danger. The facts are his. Once they have been assimilated, he exercises dominion over them as a rational being.

But the inside kind of truth can never be mastered in this way. I have called it inside because it doesn't keep its distance from us. It has a life of its own and can therefore sweep in upon us in ways we can't control. Take, for instance, something of superlative beauty – music, painting, what you will. We can indeed study and master its out-

side truth – how it is constructed and how related to what
has gone before and so forth. But its reality eludes us
altogether unless it penetrates us and evokes from us a
response we can't help giving. In this sense, far from being
in control, we are ourselves mastered by what we see. The
same of course is true of what repels and terrifies us. We
speak of being haunted by it – ugliness, brutality, meanness. . . .

Or take our relations with other people. In any society
our relations with most of its members has to be largely
impersonal. Without this impersonality, life would be
utterly impossible. If each of us were deeply involved with
everybody else, the place would be a lunatic asylum. For
other people can remain the outside kind of truth so long as
we know them only superficially. We can master the art of
dealing with them – what is called social *savoir-faire*. But
once we know them at all well, the relation is no longer completely under our control. They have a certain power over
us, whether we want them to or not. When I say, "So and so
gets on my nerves", it means that my relation to him has
become the inside kind of truth.

This sort of truth is always hitting out at me in one way
or another. It conjures up something within me previously
dormant – love, hatred, happiness, misery, fear, anger,
peace, joy. It never leaves me as I was. Always it brings a
blessing or a curse. And both are really me, aspects of
myself generally submerged and unenfranchised, now
raised to the surface and given a voice in what I am.

But extending the franchise always seems a risky business, and there is bound to be considerable opposition. And
so the temptation is strong to treat the inside kind of truth
as though it were the outside kind. We call it, naturally
enough, something rather grand – being objective. But in

these circumstances, objectivity is a funk-hole. It is an attempt to keep at arm's length realities which I fear will evoke me too painfully by making me meet sides of myself I prefer to ignore.

According to St Paul, this is what people do with God. "The world," he said, "through its wisdom knew not God." Paul was not an anti-intellectual. The point he is making is that God can never be the outside kind of truth, the conclusion of a philosophical or scientific investigation. For a cool head and a cool heart never yet led any man to know any sort of love, least of all the love which passes knowledge. Such theological objectivity is an attempt to keep God out, because his love will confront us with our full selves, and we all have our skeletons in the cupboard. This is what led Kierkegaard to say, "the theologian is the anti-Christ". Yet it need not be so. For all the really creative theologians of the Church, St Paul, St John, Augustine, Luther, Pascal, or our own Westcott – all of them realized that theological truth can never be a matter of juggling with ideas, however brilliantly. All understood that it must be found inside them or not at all. "Thou mastering me, God" – that is the ultimate truth.

"When he, the Spirit of truth, is come, he will guide you into all truth." Not by means of scientific discovery, or logical argument, or some masterpiece of intellection, but by evoking the me I've always refused to meet and enabling me to take this despised and rejected person fully to myself, breaking down the middle wall of partition. And the Holy Spirit does this within me, by means of my own character and my own experience, by means of what I am. "We are not," said von Hügel, "to think of the Holy Spirit, and the human Spirit, God and the soul, as two separate entities. God's spirit works in closest association with ours." Or in the words of St Catherine of Genoa (the creator of modern hospital work), "My me is God, nor do I know my selfhood save in him."

When people say, "Not me, not me, but God, God over there," they are trying, whether they know it or not, to escape from ultimate truth because they feel it will be too much for them. They objectify God in order to keep themselves at a safe distance. But when the Holy Spirit leads us into all truth, he will be, as Christ said, within us, not outside; within the whole of us, and not just in the Sunday-best part of us – the times when we feel pious and decent or pure in heart. For, as far as we are concerned, the chief work of the Holy Spirit is to reconcile what I think I am with what I really am, what I think I believe with what I really feel; to liberate what fear compels me to suffocate, to introduce the me I loathe and fear and cut dead, to introduce this very me to the glorious liberty of the children of God.

Consider one of the practical consequences of this. I go to the Holy Communion and experience God's love and beauty. Afterwards I find myself in a worse temper than usual or more full of desire. It probably worries me, yet this is exactly what I should expect. My communion with God has given me the confidence to accept a little more of what I am. The prayer in the hymn has been answered – "What is frozen, warmly tend." And it is only by being thus first unfrozen, that these potentialities of mine can be afterwards transformed to contribute to goodness and love. Keep them permanently in quarantine, and they will always remain my enemies – and God's.

But this makes Christ's promise very terrifying. Instruments I kept locked in a drawer have now been put into my hands, ultimately so that I can use them to create beauty and all things good. But until I've learnt how to use them, I feel much worse off than I was before, more discontented, more restless, more anti religion in its established form, more anti convention, the Spirit of Christ bringing me not peace but a sword. It's unavoidable. If what the collect calls our unruly wills and affections must be not liquidated, but made available – for only so can they be ordered aright – then I'm bound to be in for a stormy time. Most of us often refuse to allow ourselves thus to be made available. I believe that, so long as we refuse in this way, we are committing the sin against the Holy Spirit which cuts us off from the abundant life Christ promised us. It's like the talent which, for fear, the man hid in the ground.

And please notice one further thing. Because the Holy Spirit is within us, because he can be known only subjectively, only, that is, by means of what I am, we shall never feel absolutely certain that it is in fact the Spirit who is working. This is the price which has to be paid for inspiration of every kind. Is it all nonsense, after all? I suppose that's why an artist or writer is so sensitive about the reception of his work. If the critics tear it to pieces, they echo his own inevitable doubts of its validity. And that's why we too can get so hot under the collar when we are judged by conventional standards. For it is our predicament never to be able to escape the question, is it the Holy Spirit or is it Beelzebub the Prince of the devils? Did not Christ himself, as he was dying, cry out, "My God, my God, why hast thou forsaken me?" (For faith consists in the acceptance of doubt, not, as we generally think, in its repression.) And must not this show that he was facing the most terrible of all possibilities – that his critics had been right after all?

But if faith fails, this inescapable doubt – our human

predicament – will drive us into the funk-hole of objectivity, what the Bible says, what the Church says, what they, whoever they are, tell us to believe and to do; they, the orthodox experts – who crucified Jesus because he trusted the Spirit within him and not the establishment.

It is right that on Whit Sunday we should offer thanks to God and praise his holy name for sending us the Spirit of his Son. But let us not be blind to how much the gift will cost us. It is a dreadful thing to be guided into all truth. "Are ye able to be baptized with the baptism that I am baptized withal?" Yet only thus can we ever be satisfied or learn what living means. "The dove descending breaks the air With flame of incandescent terror." But this fire only threatens and hurts. It never injures. Still less does it consume. On the contrary, by this fire alone can we have life and have it more abundantly. For

> *Love is the unfamiliar Name*
> *Behind the hands that wove*
> *The intolerable shirt of flame*
> *Which human power cannot remove.* *

When we discover something of our real feelings it will often seem more like darkness than light, for our feelings will often not be the good and benevolent ones we thought they were. Yet paradoxically it is in that very darkness that God meets us and the darkness is the beginning of his light. For to see things as they are is to see them as God sees them.

---

* T. S. Eliot, *Little Gidding*, iv.

Self-acceptance

The need for self-acceptance – Christ's total involvement in our humanity – the necessity for full selfhood – the universal human vocation – God accepts us totally – gentleness with ourselves is rooted in God's prior acceptance of us – the discovery that evil is the disguised slavery of man's own hidden corruption – Jesus and the unknown self – the destruction of the false self – receiving from God what we truly are – the price of creation – Charity as acceptance.

It is the capacity to accept what I am which makes me human. To the degree in which I am unable to accept what I am, to that degree am I less than fully human. To the degree in which I am able so to accept myself, to that degree am I coming into my human heritage.

So, for instance, some people find it hard to accept the fact of their animal nature. The classic example of this was the fanatical opposition shown by many Victorian Christians to the discovery of how man evolved from animal ancestors. That controversy is now long dead. But what is accepted as a scientific fact can be rejected when it becomes a matter of private and personal involvement. Not a few people, for instance, are worried because they think, as they put it, that they are over-sexed. What in fact it means is that they cannot accept the inevitability in an animal nature of strong upsurges of instinct. And what makes them less than human is not the strength of the instinct but their incapacity to accept it as inevitable.

Others reject their animal nature by overtaxing their physical resources and trying to live as though they didn't need sleep and food and rest. It annoys them that they feel tired and worn out or that they have to stop what they are doing in order to have a meal. Here again, it is not their physical needs which make them less than human but their refusal to accept the necessity of those needs.

Others again are appalled by the violence of their aggressive feelings. Those feelings are called forth by a threat, real or imaginary. And unless that instinct to preserve ourselves by overcoming the assailant were part and parcel of our nature we should not have survived as a species in the evolutionary process. Of course what threatens us now is not an animal looking for a meal but the clever acquaintance bent on showing by his wit that we are intellectually negligible, but our instinctive response to danger is the same. And we have to learn to accept the consequent aggression in ourselves as both healthy and inevitable.

As possessing an animal nature we have to accept ourselves as belonging to a species. What we have also to accept is our unique individuality, that I am I myself, the only me, who is what he is because of countless conditioning factors which go back to the dawn of time. But to see what is meant we need take back those conditioning factors no further than a generation. My parents were people of this sort. I have inherited something of their physique and their temperament, and being brought up in the atmosphere which their presence generated has left its inevitable marks upon me, either by way of imitation or of reaction. Their circumstances were such and such. Their interests and outlook on life were so and so. We lived in that sort of place and I was sent to that sort of school, and my uncles, aunts and cousins did and do this and that.

These conditioning factors have helped to make me what I now am, with this degree of good or bad looks, this degree of intelligence and sensitivity, this degree of confidence, and so on and so on. It is useless for us to wish that we were different people who had different kinds of parents and who came from different backgrounds – more loving, more secure, less narrow-minded and the rest. Our particular past is stamped upon us from head to foot.

Many people spend a great deal of their lives resenting the conditioning factors which have made them the only Richard or the only Mary of their kind in existence. But one of the main challenges which confronts every human being is the choice to accept the past which he finds imposed upon him and which has made him unlike anybody else. Failure so to accept leads to sterile and undirected protest.

It is a good and noble thing to protest against what we believe to be morally wrong in the structure of society. Without such protest, humanity would wither away. But we must be very careful to make sure that we are not in the last resort protesting for protesting's sake. For that would indicate that we have failed in one of the most important challenges of human life – to accept ourselves as the products of our particular pasts. When we thus fail to accept what the past has made us, the defiance which we appear to throw at the world is no more than a disguise for the defiance we are throwing at ourselves.

To me the supreme example in this century of such failure to accept is Adolf Hitler. The whole diabolical apparatus of Nazi Germany, with its murder of millions of Jews, its superstition of the Aryan super-race, its attempt to dominate the world, was the product of somebody who could not accept what his past had made him, and who played upon and blew up to gigantic proportions the same tendency to non-acceptance of themselves in the German people. The result was the staging of a horrific and ruthless charade designed to persuade Hitler and his followers that they were not what in fact they were, to persuade them that they were super-men and not people whose past had left them with slightly more than average feelings of inferiority. That illusion was finally shattered in the bunker in Berlin. And as a positive force the Nazi movement had and has no future, apart from sporadic isolated outbursts here and there which amount to nothing.

By way of contrast, consider Lenin. The Kremlin, it is true, has consistently been unfaithful to its first leader, but the movement he inaugurated is still alive in Russia as the readiness of intelligent Russians to go to prison for their

convictions has shown, and Communism is still the dominating force in vast areas of the world. Lenin changed the
course of history as Hitler did not, and he was able to to do
so because he accepted himself as the product of his past
environment. What largely adverse conditioning factors
had made him, he used as his supreme opportunity.

Hitler's devilish charade was an attempted antidote
for doubt and anxiety. This reminds us that we cannot be
human unless we are willing to accept doubt and anxiety. I
say this here in case I have given the impression that if we
are able to accept our past, then life will be perpetually
serene and unclouded. It won't. From time to time we shall
doubt our capacities, we shall be uncertain whether we can
keep it up, we shall be anxious about the future, we shall
wonder whether life has much meaning or value after all, we
shall feel that nobody likes us much, we shall think of ourselves as one big promise of failure, we shall suspect that no
woman will ever love us because there will always be
another man she loves more, we shall in short feel sub-
human. To be human is precisely to be vulnerable to this
sort of inner attack. If we regard it as intolerable, out-
rageous or even unusual that we should have occasionally to
undergo suffering of this kind, then we shall only make it
worse.

Whatever you pretend to your friends, don't pretend
to yourself that you are not in fact feeling what you are. If
you accept these attacks of doubt as an inevitable part of
being human, their hold on you will grow weaker and you
will find yourself passing through them as through a temporary storm. If you don't accept them, it means that you will
worry about them, and then their hold on you will grow
stronger. And if their hold on you is too persistent, you may
find yourself putting on your own charade for your own

benefit, building up a fictitious you who is tough, or heart-less, or full of fun, or oozing with bonhomie or sensibly never ruffled, as the case may be. If you can come to believe that this stage-prop of painted cardboard is in fact your true self, then your capacity to accept would dwindle to insignificance. You would be hardly human.

In Christ, we believe, God involved himself totally in our human predicament. How then, with regard to our own selves and psychic make-up, can we refuse to do the same? And here Freud pointed the way. For he "promulgated the belief . . . that the psychological laws governing our un-conscious, affective life are equally valid for all men, the mentally ill and the mentally healthy; that these laws are not violated in health or in disease any more than the laws of chemistry or physics are different in physical health or physical disease. In other words, Freud opened the road for a proper psychological identification with the neurotic and psychotic . . . an identification based on an actual psychological equation between ourselves and the mentally ill.''* This is the involvement, the incarnation, and the cross, of self-awareness. And this is why we are tempted to forsake Christ and flee, concocting for our flight the most convincing reasons possible. We cannot bear to put ourselves in the same class as the afflicted. Yet this is also the road to resurrection, to fuller, richer life. For it is our hatred of what is buried within us, our fear of it and guilt about it, which keeps it excluded from our awareness. And it is precisely this exclusion which maintains it as an enemy felt to be working against us.

When received into awareness, it loses its power to hurt or destroy, and, in time, contributes positively to the well-being and depth of the personality. I may, for instance,

* Gregory Zilboorg, *Bulletin of the New York Academy of Medicine* (December 1956), p. 894.

have the habit of quarrelling with my friends and tend therefore to lose their friendship. It is easy for me to explain this fact as due either to something wrong in them or to my own circumstances, such as the necessity to overwork. I am too frightened to receive into awareness the buried child within me, who is terrified of losing his own identity by parental domination or possessiveness. It is this buried child who is losing me my friends, for he converts them into the dominating possessive parents with whom I have to quarrel in order to preserve my individuality.

It is painfully terrifying to acknowledge this child and to receive him into awareness, for it looks as though, once acknowledged thus, he will make havoc of me altogether. He will make me fall out completely with everybody and everything so that I shall no longer be able to live. But this in fact does not happen. Received into awareness, the child disappears. But he leaves behind something of enormous value — that instinct to be myself and to give expression to what I am, from which flow all the highest achievements of human life, whatsoever things are lovely, whatsoever things are good, of which the greatest is the capacity to give myself away in love. It is thus that I pass through involvement with an alienated self, the cross and the passion, to the glory of the resurrection.

Self, we are told, is the enemy. We must choose between self and God. Now it is gloriously true that in the garden secretly and on the cross on high Christ taught his brethren and inspired to suffer and to die. But such self-sacrifice and self-surrender is possible only when selfhood has been achieved. And it is in fact an affirmation of the self, not a denial of it. We do not abdicate what we are when we give ourselves away, as though we displaced ourselves in order that God might reign where we once reigned. The alternative between God and the self here is false.

If God is our Creator then it is by means of our being ourselves to the fullest possible extent that he reigns. For God is not our rival. He is the ground of our being. And only when we begin to reign with him in the full possession of our human selfhood can we begin also to suffer with him and to die.

The ultimate challenge of life is squarely to face our capacity for evil and destruction and by receiving and assimilating it to transform it into what is positive and creative, so that the dynamic of our evil potential becomes harnessed to what within us is constructive and good. This acceptance and transformation of our own destructiveness is the *sine qua non* of all personal growth, and it means that in some form or other the bloody sweat of Gethsemane is the universal human vocation which must be undergone by everybody who chooses life instead of death. When therefore we are tormented by rage and jealousy and hatred and envy, together with the stifling frustration and despair in which they issue, it is not, as we generally imagine, a sign that things have gone radically wrong. On the contrary, it indicates that we are indeed taking fate by the throat, grappling with our endless death-dealing past, facing ourselves as the products of causes which go back to the dawn of time, refusing any longer to keep them locked up out of sight, but wrestling with them as Jacob wrestled with the stranger, compelling them to leave a blessing behind where it looked as if there was only a curse. For these evil destructive things are evil and destructive only in so far as we attempt to exclude them from what we are and keep them at arm's length from ourselves. When we admit them into awareness, although at first they appear to wreak havoc with us and produce all but intolerable turmoil and distress, they are in fact being taken up into our constructive creative selves and contribute as nothing else can to our power for good.

Jesus told us to love our enemies, for by loving them we may turn them into our friends. This applies supremely to the enemy within. For our own worst enemy is always ourselves. And if with patience and compassion I can love that murderous man, that cruel callous man, that possessive envious jealous man, that malicious man who hates his fellows, that man who is me, then I am on the way to converting him into everything which is dynamically good and lovely and generous and kind and, above all, superabundantly alive with a life which is contagious. That is the goal to which we are being led by means of our agony and bloody sweat, our cross and passion – to our glorious resurrection whereby vitality and strength and joy are brought to others in what is truly a coming of the Holy Ghost. For by a strange transmutation the enemy of mankind within ourselves is discovered as nothing other than the Eternal Word creating us – that Word whose characteristic manifestation is invariably in the form of a figure whose wounds are his glory and whose death is his resurrection.

When through love of what I am I accept myself as a potential murderer, then I find myself capable of murdering ignorance, prejudice, suspicion, and fear. When I accept myself as possessive, jealous, and envious, I find that what I covet earnestly are the best gifts, of which the greatest is the charity which is willing to suffer and strive for the fulfilment of others. When I accept myself as hating and malicious, I find that what I hate and abhor is everything which corrupts and destroys that tender love for the men and women I know intimately, whose presence, whose very existence, is my supreme happiness and satisfaction. It is this conversion and transformation of evil into good, of destruction into creation, going on within us now as we wrestle with our fate, which is summed up and represented in the figure of the Eternal Word crucified and raised from the dead. For it is not a case of asking – "Who can go up to heaven? (that is to bring Christ down) or, Who can go down to the abyss? (that is to bring Christ up from the dead)."* For the Word is near us now in our hearts, and it is in our hearts now in the present that the Word is made flesh, suffers, dies, and is raised from the dead. That ultimate miracle is a daily and hourly occurrence as common, and from one point of view as ordinary, as mankind itself.

William James said that the fundamental keynote of his experience was always reconciliation, and his words are worth quoting as they describe with his characteristic lucidity what I have been attempting to describe: "It is as if the opposites of the world, whose contradictoriness and conflict make all our difficulties and troubles, were melted into unity. Not only do they, as contrasted species, belong to one and the same genus, *but one of the species*, the nobler and better one, *is itself the genus and so soaks up and absorbs its opposite into itself.* This is a dark saying, I know, when thus expressed in terms of common logic, but I cannot wholly escape from its authority."§

When I say that God forgives me, I generally mean that he accepts me, without reservation, as I am. He accepts the me who, because he is only part of himself and equates this part with the whole, is ugly, distorted, and subject (though largely unaware of it) to compulsive actions – that is,

* Romans 10:7.
§ William James, *The Varieties of Religious Experience* (Longmans, Green, 1952), p. 379 (his italics).

actions which, although rationalized ably enough, are in fact attempts to preserve at all costs my limited awareness of what I am. Forgiveness means that God accepts me thus, just as I am. But can this fundamental truth of the Christian gospel be more fully described?

Perhaps it can be said that God accepts me just as I am because he sees that in fact I am not just this. Perhaps he can be described as seeing below the surface of my superficial self (which I consider the whole) to an underneath where lie the materials from which a being in his image and likeness are waiting for construction. And perhaps this may illuminate St Paul's idea of Christ in us, or better, Christ being formed in us. In short, when God forgives me, he receives the self of which I am unaware. His reception of the self of which I am aware is only a necessary stage in a therapeutic process. It opens me out to what I am. Certainly this is what happens in human relations. When I act compulsively (for example, lose my temper with my friend) nothing restores me to goodness and love so effectively as his refusal to believe that the me who lost my temper is anything but a superficial and unimportant aspect of my full self. Forgiveness is rooted in this conviction. Without it, there can be no forgiveness. I cannot sincerely welcome a serpent to my bosom, but only a man temporarily strangled by a serpent. All forgiveness, God's and man's, must be rooted in truth.

Gentleness springs from the ability to accept ourselves as we are, inevitably imperfect and falling far short of any ideal portrait of ourselves we may entertain. We may indeed label such a portrait not with our own name but with that of Christ. It makes no difference. The ideal thus painted is bound to be in some degree a caricature. One of the aspects of self-acceptance consists in facing the fact that what has probably to change most within us is our notion of sanctity. That is why there is no need for our current version of it to persecute us. In spite of it, we can accept ourselves. But how? We cannot do it by deciding to. For if there is any truth in Christianity, it is certain that we are not the captain of our soul. The ability to accept ourselves can come from nothing else than our faith in God's prior acceptance of us just as we are – in whatever intellectual forms or by means of whatever human circumstances such faith may be mediated to us. For, although we believe God spoke in Christ, we also believe that the Christ in whom God spoke is the Eternal Word – the true light which enlighteneth every man. And so, whenever or wherever a man accepts what he is, it is because he has first heard, in whatever idiom, God's word of acceptance.

"It is God that justifieth. Who is he that condemneth?" It is absurd to suppose that we believe in God's acceptance of us (which is the quintessence of the Christian gospel) if at the same time we are anxious and worried about the sort of people we are. Who are we to condemn ourselves if God does not? Do we know better than he or is our standard of morality higher than his? Is it for us prodigals to play for our own benefit the part of the elder brother? Our faith in God must inevitably include and bring with it our ability to accept ourselves. And this is the spring of gentleness. God's attitude towards men, revealed in Jesus Christ, where faith is present, will find its echo in men's attitude towards themselves. A believer will be forbearing and forgiving towards himself. And he will not consider this dangerous, lax, or misleading if God's calling him his son has evoked a response of filial trust.

Harshness towards myself, condemnation of myself,

anxiety about my possible failure to achieve a standard of goodness fantasied as within my grasp, these are the signs of my lack of faith in God's creative call, signs that I am making myself into my own god. This idol, because he is a false god, is an insecure god. And because he is an insecure god, he must have the apparatus of force to maintain his despotism. He is too frightened to be capable of gentleness. For gentleness can come only from strength, and absolute gentleness only from absolute strength. It belongs alone to the Lord God omnipotent who is the Father of our Lord Jesus Christ. And in his acceptance of us as we are springs our power to be gentle with ourselves.

Straight is the gate and narrow is the way", said Jesus, "which leadeth unto life, and few there be that find it." The churches generally preach something different – "Few there be who, having found it, have the moral courage to walk on it or remain walking on it. For it is easy enough to find. It is plain for all to see." The ease and certainty with which the churches point to the road and their assumption that it is obvious to all men of good will leads me to think that the road they thus recommend is not the narrow way at all but the wide gate and the broad way which leads to destruction.

The weapon with which the churches bludgeon me on to the broad way is that of inflating the feelings of guilt which lie latent in us all. Make a person feel guilty enough and he will do what he is told. This latent guilt-feeling is a non-rational sense of a harshly authoritative figure who judges and condemns us. It is as though the external authoritative figures we have known all our lives have been injected inside us like a virus and have in this way become part of ourselves. If we think God exists, these feelings of a harsh pitiless authority get associated with him, however much our conscious reason insists that God is Love. Even if, shall we say, a man is a Christian theologian of the highest calibre, it is still possible for him to feel the inner Juggernaut, and in his feelings to confuse the Juggernaut with God.

What H. G. Wells's Mr Polly thought of God we educated people do not think of him. But there can be very few of us indeed who do not sometimes in a confused way *feel* God to be as Mr Polly considered him – "A limitless Being having the nature of a schoolmaster and making infinite rules, known and unknown, rules that were always ruthlessly enforced and with an infinite capacity for punishment, and, most horrible of all to think of, limitless powers of espial". Now it is not at all difficult to whip up this unholy ghost inside us and make him active. There is a great deal wrong with the world, and the ghost can be made to tell us that it is largely our fault. I remember a preacher making us feel that it was our selfishness which helped to cause the 1914 war, although most of us had not been born until after the armistice had been signed. But of course it is generally done with greater subtlety than that, although the object aimed at is the same, to make us feel shabby, mean, contemptible, monstrously ungrateful to the God who made us. And so the unholy ghost within us is set furiously to work.

He is what William Blake called the Nobodaddy – Nobody's daddy, he who is not. Even mild, gentlemanly, sober, cautious exhortations about sin give Nobodaddy his opportunity. In Blake's words – "The Nobodaddy aloft farted and belched and coughed." And the result is we feel it absolutely necessary to placate him. And here is the deadly opportunity for effective evangelism. We have been brought under old Nobodaddy's spell, and towards him we insinuate, flatter, bow and bend the knee. (If you want to know what I mean read Cranmer's two general confessions in the Book of Common Prayer.) But hope is offered to us. We shall be saved if we do what we are told. This may be giving up a sin or practising a virtue. It may be the performance of religious exercises. It may be singing "Just as I am without one plea", and "I am all unrighteousness". Nobodaddy's fury subsides. We have shown the white flag and capitulated to him. Peace is declared. But the peace is bought with a price. And the price is my destruction. For what I am and what I do is no longer the activity of a free agent. I am the slave of my own guilt-feelings, reduced to a puppet manipulated by this horrific puppeteer.

Let me now give you an actual example of what I have been describing. I know a man – he was a person of some academic intelligence – who was loyally practising his religion as a devout and rather High Church Anglican. One night he had a nightmare which proved to be a turning point in his life. In his dream he was sitting in a theatre watching a play. He turned round and looked behind him. At the back of the theatre there was a monster in human form who was savagely hypnotizing the actors on the stage, reducing them to puppets. The spectacle of this harsh inhuman puppeteer exercising his hypnotic powers so that the people on the stage were completely under his spell and the slaves of his will – this spectacle was so terrifying that the man awoke trembling and in a cold sweat.

After several months he gradually realized that the monster of the nightmare was the god he was really worshipping in spite of his having got a First in the Theological Tripos. And to this god he had painfully to die.

He had to accept the terrible truth that the practice of his religion had been a desperate attempt to keep his eyes averted from the monster of the nightmare. He had thought that, with many failures, it is true, but according to his powers, he was responding to God's love. His dream showed him that he was a devil's slave — his devotion and his goodness being a compulsive response to a deeply embedded feeling of guilt, and this in spite of his regular use of sacramental confession. It broke him up temporarily. But later he was certain that, although he was much less religious in the usual sense, he had been brought to the straight gate and narrow way. For life and behaviour based on feelings of guilt exclude charity. To be bullied, compelled, by subtle inner unidentifiable fear to apparent worship and goodness is to destroy the self. And without a self one cannot give. There can be no charity, no love for God or man.

The dreamer whose history (with his permission) I have recounted was seen, about two years after his nightmare, drunk among the bars and brothels of Tangier. He was learning that for him evil was not what the priests had told him it was, but rather that evil was the disguised slavery to his own hidden corruption which had led him to go to Mass every day and to confession every month. And he told me that words of Jesus rang in his ears like bells of victory — the words which Jesus addressed to the churchmen of his day — "Verily I say unto you, That the publicans and the harlots go into the Kingdom of God before you."

Now I am not suggesting that it is a good or morally desirable thing to spend one's time drunk among the bars and brothels of any city. What I am suggesting with all the emphasis at my command is that there are worse, much worse, evils than that. Worse because unperceived and thus

sincerely imagined to be good. If you are the slave of drink
or sex, somewhere inside you, you know you are a slave.
But if you are the slave of guilt-feelings, you can deceive
yourself and call it the service of God or even free response
to God's love. That is why a congregation of "good"
people in church can be much further from the heart of God
than those who have strayed from the path of conventional
behaviour. "They that are whole", said Jesus, "have no
need of the physician. But they that are sick!" . . .

I believe that behind the outwardness of much worship
and good works there lies a fact which Christians
unknowingly do all in their power to keep hidden from their
eyes – the fact that they have sold themselves as slaves to the
demon of guilt-feelings, however much intellectually they
refuse the idea and however enlightened their theology of
the atonement. For what we really believe is often very
different from what we think we believe.

There is ample evidence in the gospels that Jesus
recognized that men were the prisoners of what they would
describe as their best selves. Much of his teaching was concerned to explode the pretensions of this oppressive tyrant,
and in his place to evoke an attitude of trustful receptivity
to life, that is, to a me which is mysterious and unknown.
The very form of his teaching worked to this end. The
language of logical argument and abstract concepts confirms the oppressor in his tyranny. Such language, because
it can be mastered and the significance of its statements
exhaustively understood, is one of the chief weapons in the
armoury of the self I know. On the other hand, the
language of parable and poetry and concrete image eludes
the familiar thinking mind with its technique of putting two
and two together and leaves it asking – "What does the

parable mean? How can it be converted into the abstract concepts which can be fully defined and exhaustively understood?'' ''What is this that he saith – A little while? We cannot tell what he saith.'' ''And they were all amazed, insomuch that they questioned among themselves, saying, What thing is this? What new doctrine is this?'' For the language of concrete imagery, eluding the self I know, is capable of speaking to and thus evoking a self of which I have hitherto been unaware. And it is often in this way that the strong man armed is conquered and spoiled of his armour.

St Paul and St John continue the attacks made by Jesus upon the restless, scheming, anxious pretensions of the conscious self. Justification by faith means that a man has nothing else on which to depend except his receptivity to what he can never own or manage. And this very capacity to receive cannot be the result of effort. Faith is something given, not something achieved. It is created by God's word in Christ. St John speak of being born of the Spirit which can be controlled no more than the wind. And he insists that no man can come to Christ except the Father draw him. And the Father draws a man by the spectacle of Christ dying and dead. If the works of Jesus are seen as masterly assertions of his human will, they are misunderstood. For in fact they speak of his entire dependence on what is not his to exploit and manage. They look forward to and anticipate the surrender in death of all he owns.

However Christians may have used their Christianity there is abundant evidence in the New Testament that the Christian gospel, far from boosting the pretensions of the known and controllable self, seeks its subservience to a trustful confidence in a God who is creating what I am by means of which I am unaware.

The slow death of the false self, the self-enclosed ego, is not pleasant for anybody. It is bound to be a matter of misery and pain for all on whom it falls.

But it comes with a special poignancy on people who are religious and who sincerely believe that they have really been trying (as indeed they have) to love God. For mixed up with their genuine outgoing love for God there has been an attempt, without their being aware of it, to use God as an ally of their self-enclosed egos, the protector of the religious empire they have so carefully built up within them. And they have confused this self-made religious empire with God himself. So when God, by means of this or that, begins to break up this false religious ego-self, the devout often tend at first to be angry with the people they choose to cast as the destroyers of their faith. And then, if the process of demolition goes on, they feel left without any divine support in a state of what they imagine is total unbelief. But what in fact they have ceased to believe in is their own idea of God as the buttress of their own religious egos, and it is God who has smashed up their ideas of himself in order to destroy their false fabricated religious identities.

When . . . God destroys the false self with its false securities, he does so to make room for the true self to grow. There will probably be a time-lag between our awareness of the destruction and our awareness of what is growing, but the growth in fact begins at the very moment of demolition; or rather, the dying of this or that aspect of the false self is always a sign that we are ready to receive from God what we truly are. And the more we receive from God what we truly are, the more content shall we be for the ramshackle empire of our isolated ego to collapse. Of course it doesn't happen in a day. It is a long, costly – and glorious – process.

The self we truly are, the self which flows directly from God's continuous creative act, is a self alive with an inexpressibly rich quality of life because it is totally open (and hence totally vulnerable) to its own inner dispositions (none of which it disavows), to other people, to the truth wherever it may lead, to the created world in its profusion and variety sometimes threatening and sometimes succouring us, to pleasure – and to affliction. And in all these things it finds the God who is Joy. It is a self that knows in the deepest places of its being that nothing can separate it from the love of God, and that his love, spread abroad and, so to speak, solidified in his world, is Joy unspeakable and full of glory. It is a self that confronts the recurrent "in spite of" of human living (in spite of my misfortune or illness or of Betty's death) and swallows up this "in spite of" with the triumphant "how much more" of God's self-giving love. For God makes of a loss that is real and devastating the means of an increased apprehension of himself, which is our only ultimate gain – though that is a truth that it may take years or a lifetime to realize.

What we have described has well been called the logic of superabundance. That logic of superabundance, of God's continuous and increasing gift of himself to us, is the context in which the true self breathes and lives. Concupiscence, clutching at things (including God), is entirely absent because we can lose nothing without gaining more.

The true self, because it trusts God to do what he has promised, has no need to be tortured by the mirages our hymns frequently hold up before us of our being "perfect and right and pure and good" – mirages which are perhaps the most blatant form of idolatry to which we are tempted. The true self, because it has realized its deepest centre in

God, is not unduly perturbed to find that towards the periphery it is fragmented and messy. That is what it expects, for it is free from spiritual *folies de grandeur* and understands that it is still being created and that creation (as the scientists have shown us) is not a clean operation complete in seven days, but involves all sorts of false starts, dead ends and general mess over an immense period of time. So the true self does not bury its talents in the ground for fear. It accepts disarray as the price of creation.

Charity is not consequence. It is not reward. Charity is gift, God's gift of himself to us, the gift which makes us what we are. And we do not receive it in any specialized activity abstracted from the rest of our lives. For God gives himself to us in everything, including our own nature. In our own capacity to feel, to think, to criticize, to condemn, to love, to resolve, to endure – there is God giving himself to us, there is that most excellent gift of charity.

Charity is the power to accept, to accept ourselves and other people and the world as the presence of God. Charity is the power not to deny but to affirm experience, not to shrink away from it in frozen or indignant alarm but to go out and meet it, because, in spite of the apparent threats and dangers, it is our creator, come, not to steal, nor to kill, nor to destroy, but that we might have life and have it more abundantly.

God in all and through all

God in everything that we are – sharing in the life of
God – the daily bread of ordinary experience – only in
God's reality can we find our own – the discovery of
God as our deepest self – our true selves are one with
God's relationship to all creation.

The joy which a man finds in his work and which transforms the tears and sweat of it into happiness and delight – that joy is God. The wonder and curiosity which welcomes what is new and regards it not as threatening but enriching life – that wonder and curiosity is God. The confidence which leads us to abandon the shelter of our disguises and to open up the doors of our personality so that others may enter there, and both we and they be richer for the contact – that confidence is God. The vision which enables us to see the majesty of men, of all men including ourselves, piercing through the ugliness of the obscuring pathology to the beauty of the real person – that power of vision is God. The sense of belonging to the natural world, the exhilarating certainty that all things are ours whether things in heaven or things on the earth – that sense of belonging is God. The superabundance which leads us naturally and inevitably to give, not as a matter of duty nor in a spirit of patronage, but because we cannot forbear – that superabundance is God. The compelling conviction that in spite of all evidence to the contrary, in spite of all the suffering we may have to witness or to undergo, the universe is on our side, and works not for our destruction but for our fulfilment – that compelling conviction is God.

In experiences of this sort, which occur to all of us whether or not we are technically religious, it is as though we were receiving something, as though we were reaching forth to embrace a richness greater than ourselves. Greater implies other. Yet what we receive does not turn us into paupers who cannot work their own passage. On the contrary, it is in such receiving that we are most alive, most ourselves, most capable of great achievement and high endeavour. That is because God is the ground of our being, whose imparting of himself makes us what we are and establishes our personal identity. And because this is so, the alternative, God or man, is false. This is particularly important in these days when we are apt to think, "My experience of the worthwhileness of life, of gladness, of adventure, of communion, of love, this is not God. 'It's just my emotions, or it's just sex – something which can be explained away by biochemistry, or psychology."

Of course it is our physical make-up. Of course it is our emotions. Of course it is sex. Very much more so, probably, than we understand, or, in our stupid suburban spiritual snobbery, are willing to admit even to ourselves. Of course it is everything we are. But then, everything we are is God imparting himself to us, and therefore in everything we are we feel after him and find him. The whole of us flows from the one fountain of life, and it is by means of the whole of us that we return to the source from which we have sprung.

It is because religion in the true sense is as comprehensive as life itself that we cannot find God or serve him or love him with a mere part of ourselves – let us say, by a mere effort of will, by gritting the teeth and clenching the fist. What we most truly are in the depths of our being refuses to surrender to force – force from within no less than force from without. That is what St Augustine meant when he said that Christ's command to love God is not obeyed if it is obeyed as a command. That is what St Paul meant when he said, "Though I bestow all my goods to feed the poor, and though I give my body to be burned, and have not charity, it profiteth me nothing."

If God is within us and within everything around us, and eternity catches time up into itself, then our discovery of God requires of us no esoteric journey into some spiritual stratosphere. It is in the grit of earth that we find the glory of heaven. It is in our being robustly human that God enables us to share his own divine life.

God is always present and waiting to be discovered now, in the present moment, precisely where we are and in what we are doing. That is what we mean when we say that we live in a sacramental universe. Unfortunately we tend to treat the sacrament of our daily life, broken as it is into dozens of small, uneven bits and pieces, as something which hinders us from finding God when in fact it is the very vehicle of his presence. It is as though we were to complain that the bread and wine at the Holy Communion were obstacles to our approach to God instead of the means to it. If, as they do, the bread and wine on the altar represent all we are and do and suffer, then they show us that all our life in its manifold and often petty detail can become God's real presence with us, that it is in the daily bread of our ordinary common experience that we can discern the radiant body of everlasting life. The many things we have to do, the hundred and one calls on our time and attention, don't get between ourselves and God. On the contrary they are to us in very truth his Body and his Blood.

This is accepted without much difficulty when for the moment our world consists of people who need our help — the tramp who needs a meal, the neighbour in distress who needs a talk over several glasses of whisky, or the shy person who needs to be given confidence. We remember "Inasmuch as ye did it" and recognize God's presence. And it is no less easy when we ourselves are the people in need and others minister to us. It is not hard to recognize God in their sensitive generosity and to praise him for what he is giving us through them. Perhaps we remember

"Inasmuch as ye did it" even more when we are on the receiver's side of the counter. And what goes for personal and individual dealings of this kind goes equally of course for the public and political campaigns in which we engage. To join in public communal action to establish righteousness (which means humanness) in some place where it is denied is obviously to find God at work in his power and wisdom.

Where, however, we invariably fail to recognize God's presence is within those many occasions which are not conventionally associated with active compassion and charity. ("Conventionally" here means formally recognized, not, needless to say, unreal.) For people continually give themselves without their (or anybody else) often realizing what they are doing. Self-giving is not (thank God) confined to what are technically acts of piety or compassion. I arrive, for instance, at a party feeling dismal and dead. And there in talk and chatter I find myself mixed up with a lot of mutual giving and taking. The result is that I slowly become alive and begin to enjoy myself. A great deal of what appears in itself to be trivial empty talk – "Ghastly weather, isn't it?" "Did you hear what happened to Johnnie when he took the dog out last night?" "Betty's had her hair dyed!" – is in fact the machinery of communion between persons, the sacrament, the outward and audible sign of fellowship (a fact which people who are always wholly serious can never understand).

Perhaps at the party I drank quite a bit, but drink on its own depresses rather than enlivens me. What renewed me was the contact with others the drink helped to establish. It was my blindness of heart, my false idea of God, which prevented me from recognizing the true *locale* of the party – that it was Cana of Galilee and that it was

Christ himself who had for the time being changed the water of my existence into wine. If I were to recognize only the possibility of that miracle when I have to meet other people, I should most likely begin to find myself enjoying what at first sight looked like the most unpromising social occasion.

People often talk of obedience to the will of God as if his will were a loud and stern and foreign thing, as though God were a foreign power seeking to impose its own alien terms upon a subject people. That is because we are often the victims of the inadequate pictures in terms of which we think of God – the Victorian father, for instance, who *ex officio* is loving but who impinges upon his children chiefly as an autocrat demanding blind obedience. But, in fact, the testimony of all deeply religious people of all the great world faiths is that God is indistinguishable from my deepest self because it is only in his reality that I can find my own. True, I shall have to break out of the shell of the superficial me, smashing through those ingrained habits of thought and feeling which have been developed to keep the shell intact, and that may well involve me in agony and bloody sweat, in that dying to live of which all who have lived deeply have spoken. But the aim is not submission but discovery, and the result is not my being and doing what somebody else called God tells me to be and do. The result, rather, is the realization of who and what I really am, so that I am no longer taken in by the perversions which masquerade as myself. "For me to live is Christ," said St Paul, the Christ of whom he said that he knew him no longer after the flesh and whom he described as a life-giving spirit.

Those who have thus discovered their true selves are

invariably generous and self-giving, and that in the most practical way. For they have found that active generosity is their nature because it is the nature of the reality to which they belong. As a Christian would put it, the love of Christ constrains them. Such people show us in the clearest way possible that obedience is being what you are, and how can we hope to become human unless that is our goal?

When in prayer we meet God as another we generally have to supply him with clothes in order to feel his presence. We dress him up as Heavenly Father, Mighty Saviour, Good Shepherd, the King of Love, the King of Mercy, Pity and Peace, the forgiving Friend, the wonderful Healer, the Lover, etc. etc. etc. These clothes in which we dress God are perfectly legitimate. It is meet and right and indeed our duty and our joy thus to describe God to ourselves. For the descriptions powerfully evoke us and elicit from us wonder, love, and praise. Dwelling upon the representation of God as Father, Saviour, Friend, and so on, we are drawn into communion with him. We experience the living reality of his love, with all the praise and worship which accompany it, by means of the particular description of him, by what I have called the clothes with which we legitimately dress him.

But we have to be ready for various things to happen. When we begin praying regularly, treating it as an essential part of our daily life, we may sometimes feel that we are in love with God. The representations with which we clothe him evoke strong feelings within us and the language of being in love seems the appropriate language to describe how we feel towards him. Those feelings, of course, are not so continuous as they are when we are in love with a woman or a man. But now and then, during the time of our prayer, we may get the sense of God thrilling us through. It is something to thank God for and accept gratefully while it lasts. But it must not be clutched at or demanded. We must not try to whip ourselves up to it artificially by psychic effort. Nor must we imagine that something has gone wrong when God no longer thrills us through. For, although something of God's reality has come through to us by means of our representations of him, it is those representations which have evoked our strong feelings. And God has a habit of detaching himself from our representations of him and the strong feelings they evoke. Our marvellous sensations cease.

It is like ceasing to be in love with somebody and beginning to love them instead. And, although to love somebody is a far deeper, more real, and more permanent thing than being in love with them, it is also far more matter-of-fact and businesslike. Being in love is notoriously a matter of projection. We project upon the other our own ideal image and have slowly to discover that the other isn't like that. This at first leaves us feeling that we have lost something of incomparable value. But in fact we have lost nothing except the narcissistic reflection of ourselves. And what we have found is the true reality of the other and how worthy of love it is. There is a close parallel, often remarked upon, between the stages by which two people get to know and love each other and the stages by which we get to know and love God. In human relations the cross of love is a commonplace, *croce delizia*, as the operatic tenor sings. That cross has its counterpart in our love for God. "By love God may be gotten and holden" – true. But the surpassing glory of that love demands costly kinds of surrender.

Of these kinds of surrender the costliest has no parallel in the relation between two human beings. It consists of the entire disappearance of God as another. God is no longer the Friend I meet, the Father with whom I hold converse, the Lover in whom I delight, the King before whom I bow in reverence, the Divine Being I worship and adore. In my experience of prayer God ceases to be any of these things because he ceases to be anything at all. He is absent when I pray. I am there alone. There is no other.

If this experience persists – and is not the effect of 'flu coming on or tiredness – it means that something of the greatest importance is happening. It means that God is inviting me to discover him no longer as another alongside me but as my own deepest and truest self. He is calling me from the experience of meeting him to the experience of finding my identity in him. I cannot see him because he is my eyes. I cannot hear him because he is my ears. I cannot walk to him because he is my feet. And if apparently I am alone and he is not there that is because he will not separate his presence from my own. If he is not anything at all, if he is nothing, that is because he is no longer another. I must find him in what I am or not at all. It is difficult to put this experience of identity with God into words. It doesn't mean that God is identical with my empirical self, the self which has been highly conditioned (and no doubt distorted) by my heredity and environment, not to mention my own choices. Nor does it mean that God is identical with my ego-self with all its pretensions and selfish ambitions, the self which if intent on God says "J'attends Dieu avec gourmandise." It means that there is within me a me which is both greater than me and at the same time authentically myself. One way of approaching this mysterious fact would be by what is called the paradox of grace. The more God gives me his grace (i.e. himself), the more I am myself. The more I discover within me the greater than me the more I discover that that greater than me is authentically me.

The initial stages of this discovery demand of us a costly surrender, a much more than little death. For what is taken from us is the warm intimacy, the loving harmony, of our meeting with the other. Our prayers appear to pack up on us completely. But here, as always, resurrection follows death, and the new life is incomparably richer than the old. For when one person meets another, however deeply they are open to each other, they still remain separated because they still remain two. They are still two islands, however plentiful and wide the bridges between them. The intimacy of personal communion only partially overcomes the split between myself as the knowing subject and the other as the known object. When my experience of prayer is that of meeting God as another, the split between subject and object remains in part at least. At the heart of my communion with God as other there is separation. But God's relation to man is not hedged in by the limitations which necessarily surround the relation of human people to each other. In human relationships the subject−object split can be only partially overcome. In God's relation to man the subject−object split can be totally overcome. That is what what we call the Incarnation is about−God and man being one person, one identity. In this experience God is apprehended as what I myself most deeply am, and the experience is more real than the warmth of meeting.

It is, we believe, our final vocation and destiny that the splendour of God in us should resplendently say I am. But the first steps towards that state of identity feel very far from splendid. Our experience of identity with God is the very reverse of what could be described as an emotional experience. It has about it no compelling grandeur which sweeps us off our feet. Silencing ourselves for prayer, we become aware of our identity with God only as a dim and dull something in the background while all sorts of other things dance about in the foreground of consciousness. Yet that dim and dull awareness somewhere and somehow of our identity with God is felt paradoxically as the most valuable thing in our lives. It is like the grain of mustard seed which is the smallest of all the seeds but grows into a great tree under which others may take cover. For around that dim and dull awareness of our identity with God we begin, gradually and instinctively, to centre and selve the rest of what we are. That centring and selving takes the whole of our life here on earth and no doubt extends beyond the grave. But the important thing is for it to begin. And it will begin as soon as I have discovered the me in me which is greater than me, for it is around that me which is greater than me that all I am will in due time cluster and grow. Finding myself, I shall gradually make everything I am myself so that, in the end, everything I am is the presence and identity of God; to repeat the quotation from Dante: "In us the splendour of God will resplendently say, I am," so that God is "engirt by what he girdeth."

When encounter with God gives place to the discovery of my identity with him, what I have to surrender is most of what I am accustomed to call myself: the damaged sick self we all partly are and to which we want to cling because we are obsessively fixated on the damage and sickness; the ego-image self which wants to cut a figure and make a splash even if it be only as a holy and humble man of heart; the self which feels strongly, and since it is religious, likes especially to feel God's love thrilling it through; the self bent on making progress towards spiritual maturity; the self which enjoys the rhythm of rejection and acceptance and calls it sin and repentance; the self aware of its love for God and man – all this is the self which has to be surrendered as we slowly and dimly discover our identity with God, discover the me within me which is greater than me and also authentically me. In the end we find ourselves stripped of everything except that dull, dim, rather remote awareness that we are an articulation of God's own Being, a limb of his body, to use St Paul's phrase, or to use St John's, a branch of the vine which is himself.

Through this discovery of our true identity in God and the self-naughting which inevitably accompanies it, we become truly ourselves. And we discover that our true selves are not fixed isolated entities but are one with God's relationship to all creation. In God, we discover that we are in order that all things may be. We find ourselves caught up in God's continuous creative act as part of that act. As to be truly ourselves is to be lived by God, so God as creator puts out his own creative love as our love and our love as his.

See also 'Incarnation', pages 87–94.

New possibilities

The fear of wholeness and our redemption by the
wrath of God – repentance: a surrender to unrealized
possibilities – become as receptive as little children –
Christ present in our psychic distress – Freud, Jung
and the misuse of religion – psychotherapy as
repentance: a personal experience.

On the one hand we long for wholeness, and in so far as we do not possess it we are in a despair which, because it is too painful to recognize, we hide from ourselves by our compensatory activities. But, on the other hand, we are afraid of the very wholeness for which we long, and fight against its growth in us. That is the tragic dichotomy in which man is involved. He longs for that against which he fights. At all costs he wants what he is determined to reject. We talk of people as the slaves of money or class or drink or sex or religion. But that is the less important part of the truth. The deadly attraction of these compensatory substitutes is not so much in themselves but in the protection they give from the desire and pursuit of the wholeness of which men are terrified. Concentrate, for instance, on making money, and maybe you can stifle the fundamental but threatening desire for wholeness, or concentrate, again, on absolute orthodoxy in matters of faith and morals, and maybe you will be able to deafen yourself to your desire to accept God's invitation to heal within you what is sick and to raise up what is dead.

To want to be fully alive, to be fully without let or hindrance what I have it in me to be, such desire requires no explanation. It seems natural to us, and so, self-evident. If I have a good voice, my desire to use it in singing does not need to be explained. But the fear of wholeness and the fight against it, that does require explanation. Until we have apprehended the dynamics of this dread, we shall remain a house divided against itself.

Why, then, are we frightened of wholeness? The answer is that the more whole we are, the more capable are we of suffering. If I were deaf, I would not suffer from a road-drill outside my window. If I were blind and without any sense of smell, I could live contentedly in a gasworks. So far the point is obvious enough. But we are more than our physical senses. We are made up also of feelings which are deep, mysterious, and extremely vulnerable. Such feelings may be considered by us as too destructive to continue. I say "considered by us", but it need not be a matter of conscious decision or deliberate choice. If, for instance, the sight of blood produces within me an intolerable anxiety, a feeling too painful to be borne, then I faint. For the moment I am willing to surrender consciousness itself rather than endure the fear and stress which the sight of blood evokes.

Now, all of us have put certain elements of ourselves into permanent unconsciousness. According to those who have observed these things clinically, the infant and small child instinctively drive certain strong feelings into unconsciousness because such feelings are considered too destructive to have. Every human being is unique and therefore what is thus made unconscious differs in content and degree from person to person. But such an unconsciousing is universal. To an infant, its mother is its universe and its god. The infant depends entirely upon its mother for everything. To the infant (as with everybody always) to defy its universe brings destruction. Hence the infant and small child must be, not itself, but what mother wants. Such conformity is felt to be the *sine qua non* of continued existence.

If, to take only one example, my mother does not give me the physical tenderness and cuddling for which I crave, then in time, and to the degree in which it is withheld, I drive my longing for physical tenderness into unconsciousness. The infant is no longer its full self. It is the full self *minus* its desire for cuddling. Or to take another example, the infant when something is withheld from it may get into a rage. When parental training takes the form of ostracizing the infant when it is in a rage, then the price is too great. Thus to destroy one's universe is to destroy oneself. So the feeling of anger is driven into unconsciousness. The infant, again, is no longer its full self, but is full self *minus* its capacity for feeling angry. In both these examples, wholeness is felt to involve destruction and disaster. And wholeness thus comes to be dreaded as lethal.

Let us take another example, starting this time with a grown-up person. Why is John Smith so wet, incapable of making any decisions, or taking any initiative, just drifting with every tide? Or, to put the identical question in reverse, why is John Smith so over-assertive, always laying down the law and telling everybody what to do? Because the atmosphere in which he was brought up was hostile to his having a mind and will of his own. His parents did not want him to be John Smith, but their son, thinking, feeling and doing what they wanted. Hence he buried his capacity to make decisions and so forth, buried it deep and out of sight within himself. Otherwise, in all sorts of subtle ways, his parents would have disowned him. It was too dangerous to be himself. Hence now he either can't make decisions or is compensating for this inherent incapacity by laying down the law about everything. Here again, wholeness spelt disaster.

It is, I believe, for reasons of this kind that we are terrified of, and stubbornly resist, the very wholeness for which we also long. This terrible contradiction within our nature is not our fault — just as a man can't be blamed for fainting when he sees blood. It is not our fault. But it is our tragic predicament, common both to the priest and the people to whom he ministers. How then does Christ redeem us? How does he make us whole?

Christ, our Creator, redeems us first by his wrath. The wrath of God is his refusal to allow us to rest until we have become fully what we are. Discontent, unhappiness, suffering, are the common experience of all. Sometimes we feel them acutely. More often we are able to smother them. They hover in the wings of our personality because we don't like to see them strutting upon the stage. There are moments when they force themselves in front of the footlights and we have to take notice of them, whether we like it or not. I suspect, for example, that the heat engendered by *Honest to God* was to a large extent due to its forcing us to notice our own incompleteness. That in turn was due to our having misused traditional orthodoxy, not as a means of being confronted with the living God, but as a conspiracy to conceal from ourselves the pain of being only half of what we are. Be this as it may, unrest, doubt, the sense of apparent futility or staleness or ineffectiveness or drabness, or the sharper deeper wounds which everybody now and then must endure – these are God in his wrath, not punishing us, but refusing to let sleeping dogs lie, insisting that we be not less than we have it in us to be.

In other words Christ comes to us by means of our ordinary, common experience of living. In the heartache, the fever, and the fret, there is Christ in his wrath refusing to allow us to stay as we are, reminding us of our intolerable halfness. Whatever they believe or don't believe, when people come to us in deep personal distress, what they are complaining of is one stage or element of Christ's redemptive work within them. Let us have ears to hear what these people are really telling us: that they are starting to realize that they can't go on living without receiving the wholeness of which they are terrified.

I should say that all of us suffer from some degree or

other of neurotic stress. It can be there, without in any way incapacitating us from doing our work. It can show itself as no more than the twitch of the finger or the mouth. The analogy with physical disease misleads us. Our neurosis is a protest against our being half-people. It may be triggered off by external circumstances, but its real cause is that a would-be-stifled part of us is insisting upon recognition, and the *status quo* within is fighting back. The result is painful to bear. But it is a sign that the work of redemption is going on inside us. It is God's wrath against the me that is a pharisee in order that this me may open itself to accept and welcome the me that is a publican. Here I hope it is obvious that the wrath of God is completely identical with his love. It is not another aspect of God, but one and the same thing. God's love for me the publican is his wrath for me the pharisee who tries to exclude the publican.

It's obvious how important repentance is for the Christian. It was part of the basic message of Jesus. He began his ministry by telling men to repent and believe in the gospel. Unless, therefore, we are willing to repent, we cannot be his disciples. Unfortunately, however, words get twisted out of the straight when they are used for a long time. They begin by meaning one thing and come to mean another. Take the word "prevent" for instance. It used to mean "to go before". Now it means "to stop something happening". The word "repentance" has suffered in the same way. It has become saturated with ideas and feelings which were absent from it as used by Jesus. So perhaps I ought to begin by saying what repentance doesn't mean. It doesn't mean feeling guilty. Guilt is a form of self-hatred. And hatred never does any good and always does harm, especially when it is my hatred of me.

The trouble with a great number of Christians is precisely that they feel guilty about being themselves. This saps their vitality and makes them less effective people than the apparently non-religious. Let us therefore be clear that to repent does not mean to feel guilty. Sometimes people think it means trying to make yourself sorry for the things you have done in the past. Yesterday, shall we say, I went to a party, got rather drunk and kissed all the girls. It was really great fun, and I still feel that it was. But today I'm trying to make myself sorry about it. The trouble with repentance in this sense is that I'm not really being honest with myself. Most of what I am still approves of what I did, and this makes my attempted sorrow ridiculously artificial. Or perhaps I did something which brought unpleasant consequences: I neglected my work, quarrelled with the boss, and lost my job. I'm now involved in the tedious business of trying to get another which won't be so good. In common parlance I'm repenting at leisure of my laziness and bad temper. But it isn't repentance as Jesus used the word. When I experience the unpleasant consequences of doing certain things, my resolve not to do them again is a matter of mere instinct. The man who won't eat oysters because they always make him ill can hardly be described as an example of repentance.

But if the word doesn't mean feeling guilty, or trying to be sorry for something you enjoyed doing, or resolving to avoid actions that bring disagreeable consequences, then what does it mean?

It means, in essence, discovering something about yourself, something positive, not negative. It means realizing that you have potentialities of which you have been so far unaware. It means something within you opening up which hitherto was closed. Suppose I once used to design dust-jackets for novels. It required a certain degree of skill and imagination, and it contented me for quite a long time. Then I began to get bored with it. Occasionally it was more acute than boredom. It was a very painful, though rather inarticulate, sense of frustration. It then occurred to me that I was perhaps wasting my time designing dust-jackets. Maybe I had it in me to be a real painter, perhaps a great painter. If so, then I should have to devote myself to it completely. I couldn't go on designing dust-jackets and at the same time give myself away to the visions of beauty which seemed ready to dance before my eyes. The moment came when I knew I had to decide one way or the other. Yet, in another sense, it wasn't really a decision at all. My power to see in ordinary objects more than most men see, and to put it on to canvas, this inner power of mine gave me no rest until I had surrendered to it. I became a painter, and found a richer, more satisfying life. More painful than the old one, certainly liable to agonies unknown before, but fulfilling and infinitely worthwhile.

That is what repentance means: discovering that you have more to you than you dreamt or knew, becoming bored with being only a quarter of what you are and therefore taking the risk of surrendering to the whole, and thus finding more abundant life. I'm afraid the example I gave was a bit highfalutin – it could only happen to one man in a million. Let's consider something more common: falling in love and marrying. To begin with I'm contented to live by myself and for myself. What makes me grow tired of this apparently satisfactory state of affairs? Well, of course, it's Betty with whom I've fallen in love. But what then has Betty done as far as I'm concerned? She has evoked my hitherto dormant capacity to give myself away to another person. She has made me realize that it is only by such surrender

that I can find my full self. And since it happens that I have
done the same for her, we marry. I have to work harder now
than I used to, in order to support my family. I've sold my
car and buy my suits off the peg. But what are cars and
expensive suits compared with the love which has enabled
me to grow into my proper stature instead of being the
dwarf I was in my bachelor days?

What I'm trying to emphasize is that repentance is an
inevitable part of all human life, whether people think of
themselves as religious or not. Its root is the discovery by us
that we are keeping a large part of ourselves locked away,
and hence that we are living much more superficially than
we need. This discovery is made possible by a vision vouch-
safed to us of some good: the hidden beauty of the world in
the case of the painter, the lovely person Betty is, in the case
of the man who marries. This good, whatever it is, demands
surrender to itself. And the consequence of such surrender is
a changed life, changed because richer and deeper and more
satisfying. And this, because we are using more of what we
are and keeping less untapped.

And here perhaps we should pause to consider the
criticism which Jesus passed on the good religious people of
his day. "The publicans and the harlots", he told them,
"go into the kingdom of God before you", and "there is
joy in heaven over one sinner that repenteth more than over
ninety and nine righteous persons who need no
repentance". The religious keep their code of morals, and it
insulates them from most of what they are. In such a state,
they can have no vision, no discontent, no surrender. They
keep their talent firmly buried in the earth. They remain a
quarter of what they could be. The sinner, on the other
hand, tries to live as fully as he can, and discovers by his
frustration and despair, how intolerably confining and

cramping is the small part of himself which he identifies with the whole of him. This leads him to repentance. He keeps his eyes open for a vision of something better. When it is given to him he surrenders to it, and thereby more of what he is becomes available to him. As always, the result is joy.

But at this point the really vital question obviously is, what are the limits of our potentialities? What have we in us to become? What sort of person shall I be when the whole of me is brought into play? Christians see the answer to this question in Jesus Christ. When, in the gospels, they read of his life and teaching, they recognize themselves. Not themselves as they are, but themselves as they could be.

Take, for example, the most well-known of all the parables, the Good Samaritan. Why is it such a favourite? Because we recognize ourselves in the two chief characters of the story. When I think of what life has done to me in this way and that, especially that I can't be everything I have it in me to be, then I know I am the wounded man left half-dead and needing rescue. But I also know that I am potentially the rescuer as well. The Good Samaritan is a vision of myself. He is me with my deepest capacities no longer hedged in and constricted, but brought into play. He is me fulfilling myself by active compassion for another.

When I can be a person like the Good Samaritan and do what he did, then, I feel, I shall be fully me and abundantly alive. Now throughout his life, Jesus was himself the Good Samaritan. That is the power which he exercises over us. Jesus is the vision of me as I have it in me to become. And this vision unlocks areas of my being which have so far been inaccessible to me, and even unknown to me. I begin to discover what sort of a person I am, the sort of person who can find his fullness only in self-giving. This discovery is repentance. It brings a change of character, a new and more deeply satisfying life.

Christians claim that Jesus was God. As a matter of metaphysics this is impossible to understand. The Christological formulae of the early church councils are obscure. But behind the statement of the doctrine lies something we can all apprehend as absolutely real. Jesus is the vision of man fully himself. And man fully himself shares the life of the Creator, has the same character, engages in the same sort of moral activity. This is quite explicit in Jesus's teaching. "Be ye therefore merciful, as your Father also is merciful", "Love your enemies, bless them that curse you, do good to them that hate you . . . that ye may be the children of your Father which is in heaven: for he maketh his sun to rise on the evil and on the good, and sendeth rain on the just and on the unjust. . . . Be ye therefore perfect, even as your Father which is in heaven is perfect." What is a father, but he whose nature I share? The ultimate root of repentance is the discovery that we are sons of God, that we have it in us to be what God is like, to be alive as God is alive – by giving, by generosity, by love. It isn't, of course, something which happens to us all of a sudden. I shan't repent for good and all this morning.

The vision of myself which is the vision of Jesus (which is the vision of God) will come and go. And when the vision is absent, I shall try to implement what I am by methods which don't work, chiefly by grabbing of one sort or another, instead of by giving. And this will lead me time and time again to frustration and despair. Why, I shall ask bitterly, why has life got to be like this? But it is precisely when I am in this state, wounded and half dead, that the Good Samaritan will once again reveal himself to me, and thus show me my true identity, as though to say, "You're trying to be like this. But you can't be, because you're really like me." So I shall repent once more, and again be what I am. This will go on for the whole of our life. For we can't expect to take in something absolutely stupendous all at once. And the good news, the gospel, that we have it in us to be like God, more, to share God's life and partake of his nature, is, in the literal sense of the word, infinitely stupendous. We can assimilate it only slowly and by degrees. That is why repentance is an ever-recurring necessity for us. The discovery of ourselves cannot but continue, because our potentialities are limitless. "Beloved, now are we the sons of God, and it doth not yet appear what we shall be."

Children are not innocent creatures, as Freud, Henry James and Ronald Searle have shown us in their own ways. What is true of children is that they have no riches. They cannot trust to the character they have built up over the years. They cannot say to themselves, "I am this sort of person. I am not that sort of person." Hence they are very open to influence. To receive is for them the most natural thing in the world. For the average child, life is one long act of receiving. They have as yet no defences against life.

When Jesus urged men to repent, he was urging them to become as little children. He wasn't asking them to eat the dust. He was confronting them with the necessity of a radical change of outlook, a fundamental re-orientation of their lives, so that they would no longer trust for security in the persona they had built up – the drama of being me which I continuously stage for my own benefit – so that they would no longer trust that, but have the courage to become as receptive as little children, with all the openness to life, the taking down of the shutters and the throwing away of the armour which that entails. Without such repentance we cannot believe in the gospel, for the gospel announces that our only security is God's love for us, and if we look for security in what we have achieved we cannot find security in what is given us. Try to secure a place high up on the list and you don't appear on it at all.

Bonhoeffer, in a well-known remark, complained that the churches were offering cheap grace. I believe that in the same sense the churches sometimes tend to offer cheap therapy, presenting Christ as a sort of psychiatric patent medicine which quickly cures us of our disturbing feelings. I believe this to be theologically wrong. First, God must be loved for what he is in himself and not as a means on earth of winning heaven or of escaping hell. Secondly, there is no reason to suppose that in any individual at any particular time God is necessarily on the side of the psychic *status quo* any more than in a nation at any particular period he is necessarily on the side of the political or economic *status quo*. Indeed, since we have not yet apprehended and have not yet been made perfect, the opposite is to be expected. And, thirdly, the New Testament everywhere insists that we can know the power of Christ's resurrection only if we also know the fellowship of his sufferings. If, without our choice or contrivance, feelings arise within us which cause distress, then Christ is there in the distress itself, not to save us from the pain of rebirth but to assure us that we are indeed being born again.

To change the analogy: when, of old, there stirred in Abraham the desire to leave the city where he belonged and to travel he didn't know where, perhaps the most obvious course would have been to persuade him that he suffered from wanderlust – a disturbance of which God would cure

him. And when, after a few months, the cure complete, he
settled down contentedly once again in Ur of the Chaldees,
you could have talked of Theotherapy. But Abraham
would have lost everything – his vocation, his integrity, his
soul. He would have been the victim of the cheap grace
which is not grace.

The relevance of Christ to psychology cannot be of
any real concern to those whom God has not yet called to
receive into consciousness the darkness that is within them.
But those whose distress reveals that this divine call has
come, those people can, in Christ's words, look up and lift
up their heads, for their redemption draweth nigh. Like the
shepherds at Bethlehem, they will be sore afraid. But to
them also comes the message, "Fear not: for, behold, I
bring you good tidings of great joy. Emmanuel. God with
us."

Where Freud and Jung have been of the greatest
assistance to religion is in their having scattered the proud in
the imagination of their hearts. They have shown up a great
deal of religion as the attempt to make a cardinal virtue out
of what is in fact a radical evasion. Afraid of growing into
their full stature, people use religion as a device to justify
their being stuck in some inhibiting pattern of feeling. They
find it easier or safer to remain God's good little boy (God
being confused with some prevailing culture and its conven-
tions) than to bear the burden of making their own decisions and taking the consequences.

We have also been shown how religion can be the
instrument of obsession. The unconscious background here
is a threatening (and of course undefined) evil which can be
warded off by the relentless repetition of rites and formulae
in detailed exactness. It was Thomas Merton, the Cistercian

monk, who said that what hinders people from praying is prayer – i.e. a person's natural and spontaneous communion with God can be stifled by the grandiose structures of prayer which the churches and their spiritual pundits have built up and which become the repository of obsessions.

What Freud and Jung provide for religious people is a *via negativa*, no more radical than that provided by St John of the Cross or the sages of Zen Buddhism. Its effect is to sift reality from the images and emotions by which it is first conveyed and then confused.

The stock Christian defence against psychology is to contrast wholeness with holiness, asserting that it is to holiness not wholeness that Christians are called. But the contrast is misconceived. Full spiritual maturity generally includes complete psychological integration. It *is* true that many saints have been neurotics, but, to quote Thomas Merton once again, "they have used their neurosis in the interest of growth instead of capitulating and succumbing to its dubious comforts".

Among those who have received the benefits of psychological analysis there is no doubt that it contributes significantly towards the attainment of that glorious liberty described by St Paul as the hallmark of the children of God. The Spirit bloweth where it listeth, and it is characteristic of God to work outside the contrivances set up by men as his official channels.

It is often pointed out that repentance means a change of heart and mind. It involves living one's life on a new basis and in a different atmosphere. It is to stop going in one direction and to go in another. It is to die to what one has so far been and to be raised up to a new quality of life.

God's call to repentance can take as many forms as

there are people. There is no one standard form in which the call to repentance must necessarily be clothed. For the call is mediated through human circumstances and those are infinite in their variety. Yet in these days there is one form in which the call to repentance seems often to be heard and which may therefore be described as characteristic of our time. I am referring to the various types of psychotherapy and psychological analysis which not a few people nowadays avail themselves of. Therapy or analysis is not magic nor is it in any way a universal panacea. It should never be recommended to all and sundry as a patent medicine to cure all ills. But since a tidy number of people now avail themselves of it, it may be useful to put on record in what ways it brought one Christian believer to repentance, to that change of heart and mind to which the Christian gospel summons us all. I have therefore set myself the task of trying to describe what difference the experience of psychological analysis has made to my Christian faith. In what ways was I brought by that experience to repentance?

Two things should be made clear at the start.

First, there was no dramatic or sharply defined before and after. The change which took place (and it was fundamental) occurred slowly and at the time was as imperceptible as physical growth. It is only by looking back over the years that it can be recognized as decisive. A new quality of life cannot be acquired in a consulting-room like a ready-made suit. For not only has the suit to be made to measure, you have also yourself to be the tailor. And it takes time for an apprentice to learn the necessary skill.

At the start all is probably chaos and confusion leaving you for the time-being not knowing what to believe or think. (It is only by thus losing your life that you can begin to find it – a truth from which we tend to protect ourselves by trying to lock ourselves up in a strong-room of what we call belief.) And as well as chaos and confusion there will probably be emptiness and panic: emptiness because the old ready-made solutions are recognized as no longer service-able; and panic because you therefore feel you have nothing to fall back on. It takes time for all this to be sorted out so that things can begin to fall into place. There is no such thing as instant maturity or what Bonhoeffer called cheap grace. You have to work out your own salvation with fear and trembling because the analysis or therapy, if it is working properly, will in its initial stages strip you of all superficial and bogus kinds of assurance including what you imagined was religious assurance but which is dis-covered as only a god made in your own image.

Secondly, it must be recognized that the therapeutic process is sacramental; that is to say that God is working through and by means of it. The therapeutic techniques have no power in themselves to do anything, let alone to bring about any kind of repentance. All they can do is to unravel and unblock the channels of receptivity. What is received does not come from the therapy. It comes from the power of life itself or what Christians would call the grace of God. And even in the unravelling and unblocking it is God who is at work through what theologians call secondary causes – in this case through the therapist, his integrity and devoted skill. So throughout the process it is ultimately God himself who plucks up and breaks down, destroys and overthrows, so that he may also build and plant. In the last resort it is always God and God alone who calls to repentance.

What then, by means of therapy or analysis does God break down and destroy?

Fundamentally it is the pride of man. The more

obvious and childish forms of pride are comparatively harmless. It is when pride is at its most subtle that it stifles life. What subtle pride means Calvin described when he said that the mind of man is a factory of idols. And the dearest idol that we fabricate is an image of ourselves as a certain type of person: decent, generous, clean-living, devout, orthodox, a person of rock-like faith, a convinced Christian, a fount of holy joy and exuberance, a lover of God, and so on. So bewitched can we be by this idol, this image of our allegedly ideal self, that we allow it to dominate the rest of what we are. And the dominance soon turns to tyranny which can be of a very savage and persecuting kind.

We allow this fabricated picture of ourselves to put most of what we are in chains, to condemn and punish it so that it feels it has no right to exist. And since that is an extremely uncomfortable, not to say agonizing, state of affairs, we may lock up most of what we are in a kind of dark cellar, disinheriting and disowning it while we try to be nothing more than our own persecuting image. When that happens we shall inevitably at times deviate from the ideal picture we have so brutally imposed upon ourselves and imagine that the guilt or fear we feel as the result of our deviation and our resolve to try once again to live up to the demands of our idol is what repentance means.

Worst of all, we can call our idol by any name we choose, Jesus, for instance, or the Ascended Lord. The worst idols are invariably disguised under the best names. And we can do it, of course, with the utmost conscious sincerity. It is simply that pride makes us blind.

It is this tyrannical idol which God plucks up and breaks down by means of psychological analysis. And as its tyranny is gradually overthrown God's love for the self we have been in the habit of persecuting begins to be our own love too, love for what we now see as something very precious. As God is always ready to accept people who are unacceptable (that being the meaning of his free forgiveness) so we too become capable of accepting those aspects of ourselves which formerly we ran away from or tried to lock away out of sight – the disbeliever who is in each of us, for instance, or the person who hates God. Thus does God's love for our total selves find expression in our own compassionate love. And because our love is an expression of God's love it is a creative and transforming love.

What seemed formerly to militate against us because we rejected it is now discovered to be on our side contributing to the richness and depth of our God-given personality. To put it in the categories used by St Paul: by means of psychological analysis God has rescued us from our frantic attempts at self-justification by works of the law and has transferred us into the realm of faith in his free acceptance of us as we are. And the result, as St Paul saw, is a righteousness which by works of the law we could never have attained. We are living on a new basis in a different atmosphere, appropriating a new quality of life – precisely in fact what we believe repentance to be.

The unacceptable me whom I formerly rejected can particularize himself in all sorts of concrete ways: jealousy, meanness, malice, hatred, conceit, dishonesty, and so on. But in general portmanteau terms the unacceptable me usually takes three forms. First, it is the me who is indeed guilty of wrong-doing and who thus stands condemned by the moral law. Second, it is the me who lives in emptiness, and finding life robbed of all meaning is in a state of despair. Third, it is the me who is perpetually at the mercy of forces over which he has no control such as bad fortune or disease and who is in any case all the time heading for death.

It is this sinful, meaningless, and vulnerable me whom therapy or analysis calls from his dark cellar into the warm sunshine of loving acceptance. And its destructive energies are thereby slowly (and almost certainly unevenly) transformed into creative ones because, recognizing now *de profundis* that everything I am is fully accepted so that I can fully accept myself, I no longer need to be jealous or mean or malicious or whatever it may be (these things being the rejected me making his presence felt by hook or by crook). The beast has by the kiss of love become the Prince Charming who, far from having to be shut away, is now the very life and soul of what I am. A Christian who has experienced this release by means of therapy understands the deep meaning for his own being of the words in St John's Gospel: "You shall know the truth and the truth shall make you free" – the truth of God's unconditional acceptance of everything we are. And it is only from the existential recognition of that truth that genuine repentance can spring.

Repentance, however, includes more than a change of attitude to myself, fundamental though that is and the spring of all generous love for others. (How can I love others if I do not love myself? Charity, as always, begins at home in order that it may not end there). There will also be a change in my understanding of Christian truth. It will no longer be something merely in the brain. It will take on a three dimensional character, becoming something alive which lives itself out in us rather than a number of statements to be intellectually understood and made material for the machine within us which puts two and two together. Thought, it has been said, is always a post-mortem. It has to kill the living reality in order to examine it.

One important result of repentance is the breathing of life into the dry bones of doctrine so that they become clothed with the living flesh which we are. This or the other doctrine remains no longer something at a distance from you which you observe and inspect. It becomes part of your own essential identity. In the particular sense described there is, therefore, nothing odd in the assertion: "I am the communion of saints" or "I am the life everlasting" – though such statements are probably best avoided as their sense will almost certainly be misunderstood as a lunatic claim to be God Almighty.

Christian truth becoming thus part of myself meant that I could no longer say that I believed any doctrine of the Christian religion unless it had become truly part of what I was. Any doctrine which remained no more than "out there" became existentially meaningless although it might be intellectually interesting or even satisfying like a theorem in Euclid. But to believe truly, participation in the truth believed and identity with it in the sense described, became the *sine qua non*. Dry bones cannot speak, though they can be used as pieces in a jigsaw puzzle.

As it turned out it was two fundamental doctrines of Christian orthodoxy which began, as a result of analysis, to live themselves out in what I am: God's immanence and his transcendence. Of course as a student of theology I was familiar enough with the two terms and, from the intellectual point of view, understood reasonably well what they meant. But they were like people about whom I only had information but whom I had never met, let alone established any intimate communion with. I now began to see that God's immanence and his transcendence were my life. Both realities have grown within me together, but for the sake of clarity I will consider each on its own.

First then, God's immanence. As by means of the analytic process I went deeper and deeper within myself I discovered (I have already described it) ugly and wounded elements of myself which I had formerly kept hidden away even from my own eyes and was able to receive them lovingly, almost joyously, as one might receive a precious treasure once lost but now found. But (to continue the inevitable spatial metaphor) as I went deeper still within myself I discovered a presence which paradoxically was both me and not me at the same time. It was a reality infinitely greater than my individual identity and yet also a reality which not merely included me as a whole includes a part but which gave its whole self to be what I most deeply and truly was. I suppose it might be said that I discovered that I am both a self and a Self.

In terms of the Christian vocabulary I discovered the Christ in me and the Christ was more truly what I am than my individual identity could possibly be. Put in philosophical terms, I discovered Being Itself as the core of my own personal being. I also discovered Being Itself informing the world around, personal, animate, and inanimate. The Christ within, I discovered, is also the ultimate reality of all existing things – revealed either in his glory as in the loveliness of other people, the beauty and grandeur of the natural world, the compelling attraction of the arts; or in his passion as in nature red in tooth and claw and in human agony of all kinds.

This discovery of the God within, immanent as my own truest Self and the ultimate reality informing all things went, as I said, with the discovery of God's transcendence. At first, however, it seemed as if God Transcendent had disappeared altogether. What connection, for instance, was there between the God within and the figure at least metaphorically "out there" who, shall we say, enjoyed being serenaded? It looked as if God Transcendent had died on me. But then I discovered that I was confusing God Transcendent with the stereotyped god of conventional religion.

God's transcendence meant (as informed theologians have always told us) that any attempted description of him as One who towers above us in his infinite majesty is bound to fail and look ridiculous. The machinery of thought and language breaks down under the weight of Reality. So God Transcendent, I came to see, is the God who appears when every image and thought of God becomes meaningless. God Transcendent is the God who abides after God has died. You don't believe in God above? Then the first intimation of God's transcendence has come to you. Formerly you imagined that the water in the bucket of your mind was the ocean. Now you have discovered your mistake.

If I were asked to sum up in a short sentence what analysis has done for my apprehension of Christian truth, I would say that it has delivered me from the narrow moralistic perversions of repentance and has shown me that repentance is as wide and continuous as life itself. From our side it is growth (not going back to a *status quo ante*). From God's side it is his creative Word; "Behold I make all things new."

2

Experience Transformed

Incarnation

The fact of Christ: a model of the Divine – what Jesus
is all about – whatever is, is part of Christ – God
incarnate now and always – God in Jesus: towards an
understanding of the relation between man and God.

I believe that both what are traditionally called the Incarnation and the Atonement are models for a divine activity which is going on all the time and is coterminous with the historical order itself. The tabernacle of God can always be and has always somewhere been with men. And one of the indications that the tabernacle of God is thus with men is when good men anywhere are prepared to suffer and die for the sake of truth and righteousness.

What is called the fact of Christ, his birth, suffering, death and resurrection, I believe to be a model of the Divine for ever entering the world, for ever obscured and destroyed, and yet always uncontrollably rising anew.

As far as I can see, the essence of Christianity consists in its refusal to separate the seen from the unseen, the material from the spiritual. Or to put it positively, in Christianity the unseen and spiritual is declared to impinge upon us only in terms of the seen and material, while the seen and material is understood to become fully its own real self only when it is recognized as the vehicle or medium of the unseen and spiritual. If you separate them from each other you misunderstand them both.

And that, I believe, is what Jesus is all about. Jesus was not a superman who could do what ordinary mortals can't do, nor was he a god disguised as a carpenter. He was every bit as observable as our friend Fred.* Like Fred he could have been the object of scientific investigation, and had the sciences of genetics, physics, biochemistry, psychology and sociology been flourishing in his day, they could have given us a great deal of valid information about him. But, like Fred, Jesus also had dinner with people and talked long hours with them. A few, both women and men, got to know him intimately. They entered into deep

* For more about Fred, see pages 2–6.

personal communion with him in which all the material facts about him ceased to matter very much because his friends were in living contact with the quintessential man who was infinitely more than the man who could be described and explained. In the physical, observable Jesus they met the Jesus who belonged to the unseen and spiritual.

I think this can happen with anybody we know well, at least to a certain degree. We saw how it happened with Fred. But, if the New Testament records are reliable, it seems to have happened to a peculiar degree as far as Jesus was concerned. The unseen and spiritual shone through the material and observable with unusual clarity – so much so that it was recognized not only by the friends of Jesus but also by his enemies. That is why they had him executed, just as that is why today the Russians have banished Solzhenitsyn.

Let me say here that I do not believe that Jesus was unique in the sense that nobody else can ever be like him. If he were unique in that sense he would have no relevance at all as far as we are concerned, for he would belong to a different species. I think, however, that it can be claimed for him that he was uniquely representative. In him Christendom has seen to a unique degree what a human being most truly and fully is. In him Christendom has seen uniquely displayed what we all have it in us to be. That is why in popular Christian devotion Jesus has often been described as friend and brother. He was, in everything, bone of our bone and flesh of our flesh.

Where I think our understanding can be unnecessarily clouded is in a preconceived notion that God is one definable object and man another definable object, so that we have to show how in Jesus the two objects can be shaken together into one cocktail. Alas, on those premises, no theological barman down the centuries has ever been able to make the cocktail coalesce, however hard he has shaken the mixer. The truth is that while the mystery we call God can only be hinted at in an infinite variety of pictures, we in the West have confined ourselves exclusively to a rather narrow selection of pictures – God as King, Father, Judge, and so on – in all of which God appears as another person.

It is here that the religions of the East have come to our aid with alternative sets of pictures – though these alternative sets were always known to the Christian mystics. There is, for instance, one particular key-picture of God which describes him as the fount or source from which we continually flow. As variations of this particular key-picture, God can be described as the ocean of which I am a wave, as the sun of which I am a shaft of light, as the tree of which I am a branch. In this set of pictures the divine and the human, God and man, are not two different objects. The human is indeed derived from the divine, man is indeed derived from God, but in such a way that God is present and active in what man is, so that man would simply not be man unless God were so present and active in him, just as the wave would not exist without the ocean, the shaft of light without the sun, or the branch without the tree.

Jesus was intellectually and sociologically conditioned by the Jewish religion in which he was brought up. In that religion the pictures in terms of which men thought of God were all pictures of a person. These were not less valid nor less true than other types of pictures, they were simply different. (In passing we might note that a parallel here for what superficially look like mutually exclusive pictures can be found in natural science when something, say an electron, can be described both in terms of particles and in terms of waves.) Of the pictures of God as a person of one sort or another, the picture which seems to have meant most to Jesus was that of God as Father. As with people, so with pictures of God, it can be said that by their fruits ye shall know them.

If Jesus pictured his relationship to the ultimate mystery which encompasses us all in terms of a son's relationship to his father, then we have only to look at his life and teaching, to the sort of man he was, to see the reality and truth of the father-picture. It upheld him in his hour of bloody sweat when in Gethsemane he prayed: "Abba, Father." Yet, for all this, the picture of God as Father had none the less only a relative, not an absolute, validity. For what else is shown by the cry from the cross – "My God, my God, why has thou forsaken me?" Here we see the picture of God as Father smashed to pieces. In the ultimate pain of that final hour the picture of God as Father became for Jesus no more than strips of broken canvas. Perhaps his final cry – "It is accomplished" – shows him to have passed beyond the God of the pictures. For no one picture of God can be absolute. If you treat it as absolute you turn it into an idol, for all pictures of God, including mental ones, are human artefacts.

Interestingly enough, St John's Gospel shows us Jesus during his ministry using the Jewish father-picture itself to give expression to something very like the wave-ocean, sun-shaft-of-light, tree-branch set of pictures. He says two things which in terms of the Jewish picture contradict each other, but which together perfectly express the truth that the wave-ocean pictures were painted to convey. "I and the Father are one", said Jesus. And he also said: "The Father is greater than I." There is no need to enlarge on how the wave-ocean, sun-shaft-of-light, tree-branch pictures illuminate these two sayings and make sense of both together.

"I and the Father are one"; "The Father is greater than I." I believe those two sentences to be true of us all, and I believe that to a unique degree Jesus revealed to us this truth about ourselves. The trouble is, of course, that, to a greater or less extent, we don't believe it, we refuse to ·realize it, we remain blind and deaf to it, because we are too busy, which generally means too frightened, to go down deep within ourselves and find God there. It is my failure thus to assimilate the truth that I and the Father are one which fixates me on a superficial level of myself and drives me to protect that superficial self by tooth and claw. All evil springs from my refusal to discover who and what I truly am, my failure to realize that I and the Father are one.

Yet it is precisely this truth – that I am a wave to God's ocean, a shaft of light to God's sun – that I apprehend, albeit for the most part unconsciously, when I deeply enjoy Fred's company, or am taken out of myself by a Beethoven symphony, or laugh hugely at what is shatteringly funny. For in each of these experiences I have a sense of belonging to a far larger world than the straitjacket world of weight and measurement, the world which can be scientifically investigated. In each of these experiences I find myself belonging also to a world which is unseen, to a spiritual dimension, to what, for convenience's sake, people have summarized by the three-letter word "God".

But – and this is the absolutely crucial reason why I am a Christian – this larger world, this infinitely large world of the unseen, of the spiritual dimension, what we call God, can be known and experienced and enjoyed only through and by means of the seen and material and tangible world, the world which science can unfold and explain to us. God is not an escape from what is genetically, biochemically, psychologically and sociologically conditioned. He is not an escape from myself as conditioned in these ways.

The empirical world is no illusion. It is real, and we destroy ourselves if we fail to recognize its reality and imagine that we can float up to the Infinite and leave the empirical world behind. We can't, because it won't leave us behind. We belong to it indissolubly. But it is precisely in and through the empirical world that we meet God and have communion with him. It is in the seen that we meet the unseen, in the material that we meet the spiritual. The heroism, the youth, the magnificence of life and death which Forster met in the Fifth Symphony came to him by means measurable by sound-waves. The transport of liberating laughter came to us by means of something which visibly happened in the visible world. And love, the greatest and most real of all realities – so much so that the New Testament says that God is love – doesn't love always come to us embodied – in Jill or Jack or parents or friends? Heaven is not somewhere else. It is earth seen for what it most truly and deeply is. For us, the only Eternal Word is the Word made flesh.

Christ is the totality in whose being everything is gathered together and revealed as one. When Christian orthodoxy affirms that in Christ you find perfect Godhead and perfect manhood united in one person what at least it is saying is that there is no life or experience or power or reality of any kind whatever that is excluded from his identity. Whatever is, is part of Christ.

That may seem strange when you think of the negative and destructive forces by which we are surrounded. How can hatred, cruelty, despair and so on be part of Christ and included in his identity? But the New Testament, in strange and straining language, speaks of Christ becoming sin for us. It speaks of him taking the form of a slave, subjecting himself to Adam's curse, agonizing so that his sweat was as it were great drops of blood falling upon the ground, suffering in a violent death the final onslaught of destructive evil.

Evil is the perversion of life. Destructiveness, for instance, is the perversion of creativity. It's those who have evaded the challenge to create who set out as a substitute to destroy. The raw material of hatred is the capacity to love. Love plus rejection which means love plus pain generally equals hatred.

The language of the New Testament suggests that Christ, by being willing to receive and to take upon himself as his own all the perversions of life, changed their character, straightened out their crookedness, made them once again the raw material of goodness. Of this the visual representation is the central Christian symbol of the cross. That gallows on which an utterly good man was murdered at the age of thirty-three is the place where we feel most loved, most accepted, most capable of ourselves doing good. Hence one of the earliest Christian hymns speaks of sweetest wood and sweetest iron while the New Testament speaks of Christ's death as a ransom as though the potentiality for good which is everywhere had been brought back from the perversions to which it was enslaved. And Christian faith sees everything in the light of that ransom. When, for instance, Dr Martin Luther King was shot dead, Christ was present not only in the heroism of the assassinated leader but also in the hatred and violence of the assassin, for it was that very hatred and violence that Christ took upon himself at Calvary, unravelling its hideous knots and using it to show what love means.

So the point still stands: whatever is, is part of Christ. Just as a person's physical body is both the vehicle of his presence and in some way or other identified with him, so everything in heaven and on earth is the vehicle of Christ's presence and in some way or other identified with him. The birth of a child, the lilies of the field, Solomon in all his glory, the infinite expanses of outer space, the violence of a mob, the assassin's bullet, the sweet warmth of friendship, the tortured man's despair, the tenderness of human love and the cruelty of human hatred: in all these places Christ is present, they are the vehicle of his real presence, preserving, rescuing, unravelling, healing, converting, transforming.

There is no place of any kind whatsoever within us or outside where the Redeemer is not redeeming and where the Saviour is not saving. Bishop Westcott once said that in St John's Gospel the story of the Passion is set out as a revelation of majesty. That revelation of majesty is present with us at all times and in all places whatever happens. That is Christ's achievement, that he has gathered everything to himself both of good and of evil so that in all, had we but the eyes to see him, we might behold the fair beauty of the Lord. Perhaps therefore the only prayer we need ever pray is that of the blind beggar, "Lord Jesus, that I may receive my sight".

Somewhere inside us there is a person who wants to give himself for the good of others. We can smother that person by self-concerned anxiety or the search for pleasure, but he is always there, ready to poke up in the most unexpected people. Doubtless we meet God when unexpectedly we meet our own feelings of generosity, but the God thus met is pretty elusive and may vanish as quickly as he appeared. It is only when we actualize our generous feelings in concrete, particular material action that heaven is established in our midst. When we meet the hungry and feed him, the thirsty and give him drink, the stranger and take him in, the naked and clothe him, the sick and visit him, the prisoner and go to him, it is then and only then that our generosity is the medium of God's presence in the world. For the Word must be made flesh, and to be made flesh is to engage in particular concrete action.

But we are not only individuals. We belong to a social order, a world order, and it is in terms of this social and world order that we must see to it that the hungry are fed, the sick attended to, and so on. It is here, obviously, that Karl Marx, though not of course himself a Christian, has contributed enormously to our understanding of Christianity. In bringing to light the economic forces which govern society and the ideological by-products of these forces, Marx, without intending to, has made it less and less possible for Christians to believe that the Word need not or should not be made flesh in terms of economic and political action. Christians are now very far from content to support any *status quo* on principle, including, let us note in passing, the trade-union-dominated *status quo* in our own country, or, for that matter, the student-power *status quo* established in some at least of our universities.

Perhaps it sounds as if we have come down to earth with a bump. But in fact we have never left earth. I am a Christian because I believe that the tabernacle of God is with men, that God is to be found in earthly friendship and love, in earthly beauty, when we laugh at the constrictions of our earthly lot, and when we work, both through private individual effort and through political action, to make this earth a better place for all men to live in. It is in these terms that I understand the central Christian affirmation: ''And the Word was made flesh." I believe in God's Incarnation. I believe that God is incarnate now and always, here and everywhere.

In the bad old days of Anglo-Catholic triumphalism there was a standard joke which used to be told about a church over whose plain and unadorned Holy Table was painted the text: "He is not here. He is risen." The joke sprang, of course, from proprietary pride in what was considered religious truth, the kind of proprietary pride which, fortunately, is less common today than in the past. But few, if any, of those who told the joke could have been aware that it had been anticipated by Hegel who directed it against Christianity as a whole, Catholic as well as Protestant. In Christianity, Hegel thought, the union between man and God was felt to be remote both in time and place because the locus of that union was fixed in the historical figure of Jesus Christ. Nothing could be done about the remoteness in time, but in the Catholic Europe of the Middle Ages people did try to do something about the remoteness in place. For did not crusaders and pilgrims travel to Jerusalem? But what, when they got there, were they able to lay their hands on? They could lay their hands only on the abandoned *grave* of their Godhead.

I am not competent to understand, let alone to expound, the philosophy of Hegel. I have repeated his bitter joke because it provides an approach to what has obviously become the major task of Christian theology during the second half of the twentieth century – a radical reappraisal of traditional Christologies and an attempt to think out afresh what is the form in which we can most adequately express the relation we believe to exist between man and God.

I am aware that in attempting to contribute to this enterprise I am bringing coals to Newcastle — if Oxford will forgive the comparison. My comfort is that at least here my poor scuttle of coals will not be mistaken for an infernal machine.

Hegel's joke emphasizes something important for Christology — namely that in all Christological discussion due account should be taken of the fundamental difference there is in character between information about Jesus on the one hand and knowledge of God on the other. Failure to distinguish between these two kinds of knowing leads to unsatisfactory results.

If we confuse information about Jesus with knowledge of God, then God becomes a transient episode in human history. He was, once upon a time, here in this world, but is here no longer — which was the point of Hegel's joke. If, on the other hand, we confuse knowledge of God with information about Jesus, then Jesus finds a place in our religious thinking and feeling only as God. As Karl Rahner has said: "It cannot be denied that in the ordinary religious act of the Christian, when it is not referred precisely to the historical life of Jesus by way of meditation, Christ finds a place only as God. We see here the mysterious monophysite undercurrent in ordinary Christology."

What Rahner describes as the monophysite undercurrent accounts for the uneasiness, if not suspicion, which devout Christians often display towards historical criticism of the gospels. Like most people they find it easier to pray to a God they can imaginatively visualize, and Christ becomes for them the imaginative visualization of their experience of communion with God. There is nothing wrong with this; it is a basic form of Christian devotion. But what we have to notice is that it is still as God that Christ is approached, not as a man. The result is that the demand is made upon the historical critic that he provide about Jesus of Nazareth only such evidence as will keep the imaginative visualization intact. In other words, the demand is made that our knowledge of God, our communion with him in terms of our imaginative visualization, be translated into information about Jesus – what manner of man he was, the total generosity of his self-giving, and so on.

It is, however, epistemologically illegitimate thus to translate our communion with God, our present knowledge of him, into information about Jesus as an historical figure of the past. For the translation confuses two different and distinct kinds of knowing. This confusion leads either to Godhead swallowed up in manhood so that Godhead, after thirty-three years on this earth, leaves it and ascends into heaven; or, more often, to manhood swallowed up in Godhead when, approaching Jesus simply as God, we demand of this historical figure that, while remaining historical in a formal sense, he should none the less only supply what can give appropriate imaginative expression to our present experience of communion with God.

This monophysite conclusion is generally hidden from us because of the ambiguity which surrounds our use of the word "Christ". We can mean by it either Jesus of Nazareth or we can mean God, and it is easy for us to avoid deciding which of these two senses we are using.

That is the nettle which the historical critic, when true to his trade, feels compelled to grasp. He sets himself to be concerned not with his present experience of communion with God, but only with the historical figure of Jesus of Nazareth. Should his researches compel him to conclude that our certain information about Jesus is too scanty for us to know anything much about him, the critic's communion with God can remain unimpaired. This can be the case even if, like Albert Schweitzer, the critic thinks that what we can and do know about Jesus shows him to be a figure so grotesque that we have nothing in common with him. Which of us, I wonder, could claim a knowledge of God so deep and so productive as good as Schweitzer's?

What I have attempted to describe is an epistemological confusion, a confusion between two different ways of knowing, which lies, I believe, at the heart of much Christological discussion, ancient and modern – the confusion of knowledge of with information about.

It is true that with regard to a contemporary human being our information about him may well be the first and indeed necessary step towards our communion with him. But with regard to an historical figure we can *only* have information about him. We cannot have communion with him because we never meet him. If we have a record of his thought, then our assimilation of it may provide us with a certain limited communion with him, but it remains severely limited. Few of us would be rash enough to claim that we were in communion with Plato or Shakespeare, especially since living writers or teachers, when we meet them, often turn out to be quite different from what their works had led us to expect. For a teacher of the past we have to depend almost entirely on information about him. On the other hand God is not an object of knowledge about which we can collect information. To imagine that he is would be to reduce heavenly things to the dimension of earthly or, in other words, to make God into an idol. That may sound strange in view of creeds, scriptures and religious traditions, but these, strictly speaking, do not provide us with information about God. They tell us of men's alleged experience of communion with God, and, unless we

verify them by allowing them to lead us to a similar communion, they remain religiously no more than a dead letter –
information about Amos or St Paul, or what have you.
Religion bids us taste, not inspect.

I am suggesting that Christological discussion has been
unnecessarily clouded by the confusion of information
about with knowledge of or communion with. The result is
that we are supposed to have communion with as well as
information about the historical Jesus, and we are supposed to have information about as well as communion
with the mystery of the Godhead. The Jesus of Nazareth I
read of, at least between the lines, in the gospels is supposed
to be my Lord, my God, my All, and I am supposed to
know as a matter of certain information that between AD1
and 33 the infinite Godhead walked this earth as he has
never done before or since.

Such belief can only be paraded in the defensive
glamour of paradox. Yet even the word "paradox" is itself
here misused. We may have to express the wealth and
subtlety of our experience by two statements which are
apparently contradictory. That is paradox. But the experience so expressed must be a present, first-hand experience.
It cannot include an estimate of events in the past of which
we have no experience at all. In those circumstances what
we have is not paradox, but simple contradiction, as though
irrationality were itself a virtue.

But what, then, is the alternative when we try to think
out afresh the form in which we can most adequately
express the relation we believe to exist between man and
God? For it is that relation, I suggest, which is of the
essence of Christology.

One thing I believe to be crucial. We must in our discussion confine ourselves to one single way of knowing, and

that must be the way of knowledge or of communion with. For knowledge of or communion with is the common factor in our relationship both with men and with God. We can have communion with our contemporaries and we can have communion with God, and the one type of communion can lead quite naturally to the other.

When I enter into communion with another human being I discover that he is infinitely more than a definable entity. At the heart of his being I find mystery, mystery which I can enter into and share, but which can never become intellectually possessed and processed as information. My entry into the mystery of another person enables me to enter into the mystery of my own self. At this level of personhood (both the other's and my own) the relation between the human and the divine, between man and God, is not one of clear-cut distinction. We find ourselves here in an area where God is both other than I am and also the same. For God is apprehended as the source from which I continually flow, and the source cannot be separated from that which continually flows from it. As between myself and God identity and difference are experienced not only as opposites but also as the same. So, in my deep communion with the mystery of another person and in the mystery of my own being, what I find is God. "The origin of religion", said von Hügel, "consists in the fact that man *has* the Infinite within him", for God gives himself to men "only as he gives a self to them". And von Hügel quotes his favourite St Catherine of Genoa: "My me is God, nor do I know my selfhood save in him."

Entering into the mystery of another person and into my own, I discover the presence of God. I discover from my own experience that the tabernacle of God is with men, and the Incarnation is revealed not as a past event of two thousand years ago, but as a contemporary present reality, a reality which involves true paradox but not contradiction, and which has about it all the simplicity of what is really profound. Emmanuel, God with us, is the meaning of the Incarnation, and God is with us now in the flesh – my own and other people's.

Is it possible to understand the New Testament witness to Jesus in these terms? Can we expound the first Christian confessions along these lines, confining ourselves to the one single way of knowing which is knowledge of or communion with?

Admittedly such an attempt can be no more than highly speculative. Translating one idiom into another is like trying to express sound in terms of colour. There is no established system of correspondence. Yet what option have we but to try? For the first Christians appear to have thought and felt in Jewish categories which, with the best will in the world, we simply cannot make our own. It looks as if apocalyptic was their gateway into faith, and that cannot possibly be ours because apocalyptic is not in our blood. For us it can be no more than a strange and alien way of thinking, still more of feeling, and so we must translate it into what we know and feel at first hand, into something of which we have living experience.

Let us suppose, then, that the original disciples of Jesus passed from information about a contemporary to communion with him. Their communion with him led them to discover what lay beneath the surface of his human identity, led them to discover the ultimate mystery of his personhood where the human and the divine, God and man are inextricably one. At the centre or inmost self of Jesus they found the encompassing mystery of Godhead. But this discovery about Jesus led them in time to discover what lay beneath the surface of their own human identities where they found the same mystery of Godhead at the centre or inmost self of their own being. In Jesus, we could say, they saw that man's relationship with the Divine belonged to a sphere in which self and not-self, identity and difference, were combined. But since for them Jesus, as a contemporary, had been the agent of that discovery, they interpreted their experience of Godhead within them in terms of Jesus, or the spirit of Jesus, within them.

So, later, St Paul, in describing his experience of relationship with God, spoke of it explicitly as one in which identity and difference were combined, and the discovery of this combination looks as if it had a central place in what we describe as his conversion. "I live," he said, "yet not I, but Christ who dwelleth in me" – a phrase ("I yet not I") which has its counterpart in most of the great religions of the world, even Islam if we include the Sufis. It expresses the experience of a Being at one and the same time greater than the self and identical with it: "Great enough to be God, intimate enough to be me".

Perhaps, therefore, what for us could best sum up the relationship of the first disciples to Jesus of Nazareth is Plato's description in the *Phaedrus* of how a loved-one "sees *himself* in his lover, as in a glass, without knowing who it is he sees". What was true of Jesus the disciples came to see as true of themselves. They too, like Jesus, were sons of God, and Jesus, as the agent of the discovery, was thought of as the mediator of the sonship.

Is there anything distinctive in the specifically Christian form of the experience of God as "I yet not I"? I believe that there is. It is what St Paul described in such phrases as "suffering with Christ", "being crucified with Christ", "being raised from the dead with Christ". Here, of course, we have to speak mythologically. For Christians the Being who is "great enough to be God and intimate enough to be me" is experienced not only as living in an eternity of unchanging bliss, but also as for ever conquering some aboriginal foe. Sharing the divine life is therefore experienced not only as living in the peace which passes all understanding, but also as sharing in the process of the divine conquest and in its cost. That, first of all, gives ultimate significance to all moral effort. And, even more important, it gives an ultimate authenticity to suffering which is felt not as senseless waste or some illusionist trick, but as part and parcel of the costly conquest by which God is for ever himself. In terms of time that conquest is perennial. It takes place in men and women at all times and in all places, and they become aware of it as they discover their ultimate identity in God.

But what, then, of that sacred word "particularity"? When I was a student theologically interested people tended to mouth the phrase "the scandal of particularity" as though it were an incantation. The phrase always reminded me of politicians trying to exhibit their failures as the evidence of their success. Let me say that I recognize the necessity of particularity, but I fail to see how it must be a scandal. The Incarnation of God is not a general, undifferentiated atmosphere. It is concrete and particular because it is found in people, and people are always particular people involved in particular events. So it is always in the particular that we find God's presence and activity. But the point I have been trying to make throughout is that our knowledge *of* God incarnate can only be in terms of those particular people who are our contemporaries and whom we can therefore know at first hand. For what can enter into our experience is not a God incarnate there yesterday, but a

God incarnate here now today. The kingdom of God, we could say, is within us, and within us now.

Such an understanding of the Incarnation is not so alien to the main stream of the Christian tradition as it may sound. Did not the author of *Ephesians* speak of "one God and Father of us all, who is above all and through all and in all"? And when down the Christian centuries we hear refrains like "Christ in us, Christ in all men", what does the word "Christ" mean but God himself at one with mankind? We can notice, too, that when the ancient fathers of the Church said that in Jesus Christ the Eternal Word took to himself not *a* man but human nature, they were at least unbolting the door for the view that God's Incarnation was not confined to the single individual person who was Jesus of Nazareth. The fathers, it is true, denied the existence of that single individual person as a human person and thought of his human nature as something new inserted into the temporal series. But the source and dynamic of their speculation was their present experience of oneness with God, and of the eternal conquest by which he is for ever himself. That, we might say, is what Christ for them ultimately stood for.

But finally then, what of Jesus the man, the historical figure of two thousand years ago?

Here, I think the possibilities should be kept as open as they can. If, for instance, we haven't much historical sense, and, like St Bernard or the Spanish St Teresa, it is natural for us to clothe our communion with God in the form of an intensely felt devotion to Jesus, there is no reason why we should not do so. There must needs be analogies of feeling just as there are analogies of thinking. And our response to God's attractiveness may well be felt analogically in terms of our response to what is humanly lovable. That is why

The Song of Songs has its permanently valid place in the library of Christian devotion.

On the other hand, people of a different temperament will so reconstruct the life of the historical Jesus as to find in him a representative expression or paradigm of what it means to live truly, meet all life's challenges without evasion, and thereby discover the abiding reality which lies behind the changes and chances of our mortal condition. Jesus is here presented as one who in all he did and said and suffered showed us the true meaning of life and death as set in the ultimate context of eternity.

Or again, there are people (as we have already noticed) whose conscience as critical historians either will now allow them to know much that is decisive about Jesus or will lead them to conclude (as Schweitzer did) that they can and do know enough about him to find him wholly unacceptable. In thus being forced to abandon the historical Jesus there is no need for such people to abandon the truth of Godmanhood. Although they are unable to find it in a figure of the past they can find Godmanhood in contemporary people, as by communion with others and themselves they discover the mystery of Godhead as the root of human identity. Devoted to actual people they meet instead of to a largely imaginary Jesus, it could be claimed for them that they have understood the cooling common sense of the Johannine utterance: "If a man loves not his brother whom he has seen, how can he love God whom he has not seen?" Or as the preacher puts it in John Steinbeck's novel *The Grapes of Wrath*: "Don't you love Jesus? Well, I thought and thought, and finally I says, 'No, I don't know nobody name' Jesus. I know a bunch of stories, but I only love people.' "

The epistemological confusion which underlies much Christological discussion has had, among other things, the effect of hiding from us what for mankind is the sheer naturalness of God. God for man is not an alien reality or a foreign power. He is more truly us than we are ourselves. That does not mean that we are as fully God as he is himself. If I and the Father are one, it is still true that the Father is greater than I. Yet, at the same time, we cannot locate Transcendence as if it were not here but somewhere else, not now but some other time. For Transcendence means, in the words of St Bonaventure, that God has his centre everywhere and his circumference nowhere. That is how he is more truly us than we are ourselves.

God appears, and God is light,
To those poor souls who dwell in night;
But does a human form display
To those who dwell in realms of day.

Because life is stronger than logic there have been countless multitudes who have shared Blake's vision and seen God around them and within, for all their apparent intellectual obedience to the doctrine of the one unique hypostatic union. Sometimes, indeed, we can actually observe the truth, like new wine, bursting through the old definition, as when, for instance, Hopkins sees a man acting –

in God's eyes what in God's eyes he is –
Christ. For Christ plays in ten thousand
places,
Lovely in limbs, and lovely in eyes not his
To the Father through the features of men's
faces.

His life is ours

Wilderness The wilderness belongs to us.
Gethsemane No escape, but victory through
acceptance.
Cross The cross is our story – a warning against
evasion – reality is on our side – inner agony
transformed – the cost of forgiveness – "My God, my
God, why has thou forsaken me?" – a true
understanding of failure and faith – evil overcome.
Death and Resurrection Both past event and present
experience – sharing in Christ's death and
resurrection – Christ's risen manhood and the
conquest of time – cult-idols, the Eternal Word and
the present experience of resurrection – resurrection
here and hereafter.

Wilderness

It is a pity that we think of Lent as a time when we try to make ourselves uncomfortable in some fiddling but irritating way. And it's more than a pity, it's a tragic disaster, that we also think of it as a time to indulge in the secret and destructive pleasure of doing a good orthodox grovel to a pseudo-Lord, the pharisee in each of us we call God and who despises the rest of what we are.

But this evening I don't want to speak about the disguised self-idolatory which will be practised in our churches on Ash Wednesday. For Lent is supposed to be the time when we think of Jesus in the wilderness. And the wilderness belongs to us. It is always lurking somewhere as part of our experience, and there are times when it seems pretty near the whole of it. I'm not thinking now of people being ostracized, or without friends, or misunderstood, or banished in this way or that from some community or other. Objectively, as a matter of actual fact, these things happen to very few of us. Most people's wilderness is inside them, not outside. Thinking of it as outside is generally a trick we play upon ourselves – a trick to hide from us what we really are, not comfortingly wicked, but incapable, for the time being, of establishing communion. Our wilderness, then, is an inner isolation. It's an absence of contact. It's a sense of being alone – boringly alone, or saddeningly alone, or terrifyingly alone. Often we try to relieve it – understandably enough, God knows – by chatter, or gin, or religion, or sex, or possibly a combination of all four. The trouble is that these purple hearts can work their magic only for a very limited time, leaving us after one short hour or two exactly where we were before.

As I said, our isolation is really us – inwardly without sight or hearing or taste or touch. But it doesn't seem like that. Oh no. I ask myself what I am isolated from, and the answer looks agonizingly easy enough. I feel isolated from Betty whom I love desperately and who is just the sort of woman who never could love me. And so to feel love, I think, must be at the same time to feel rejection. Or I feel isolated from the social people who, if noise is the index of happiness, must be very happy indeed on Saturday evenings. Or I feel isolated from the competent people, the success-boys who manage to get themselves into print without getting themselves into court. Or I feel isolated, in some curious way, from my work. I find it dull and uninviting. It's meant – it used – to enliven me and wake me up. Now it deadens me and sends me to sleep. Not, in this case, because I'm lazy, or thinking of tomorrow's trip to London, but because it makes me feel even more alone. Or I feel isolated from things which once enchanted me, the music I play, the poetry I read, the politics I argue about. I go on doing it now as a matter of routine, not in order to be, but in order to forget, to cheat the clock. The L.P. record will take forty minutes if you play both sides, and then it will be time for tea.

Or perhaps I've been robbed, robbed of my easy certainties, my unthinking convictions, that this is black and that is white, and Uncle George was a saint, and what they told me to believe is true and the opposite false, and my parents are wonderful people, and God's in his heaven and all's right with the world, and science is the answer to everything, and St Paul was a nice man, and there's nothing like fresh air or reading the Bible for curing depression – fantasies, like children's bricks, out of which I thought I should build my life, and which now have melted into air, into thin air, leaving me with nothing. Out of what bricks, then, I ask in despair, am I to build? Is it to go on always like now, just – tomorrow and tomorrow and tomorrow – a slow procession of dusty greyish events with a lot of forced laughter, committee laughter, cocktail laughter and streaks of downright pain?

But what I've been describing is the true Lent, the real Lent, which has nothing to do with giving up sugar in your tea, or trying to feel it's wicked to be you. And this Lent, unlike the ecclesiastical charade, this sense of being isolated and therefore unequipped, is a necessary part, or a necessary stage, of our experience as human beings. It therefore found a place in the life of the Son of Man. Because he is us, he too did time in the wilderness. And what happened to him there shows us what is happening to ourselves. Here, as always, we see in his life the meaning of our own.

What then happened to Jesus in the wilderness?

I believe that in the later gospels the story has been written up. It looks to me like a sermon from an early Christian preacher, one of the greatest sermons ever delivered. But, even so, it can't compare with the stark simplicity of our earliest record. Here it is, and in this case at least St Mark tells us more by being less talkative than St Matthew and St Luke. At his baptism in Jordan, the Spirit of God had descended upon Jesus, and in his heart there rang an immediate certainty of being chosen to do great things – "And there came a voice from heaven, saying, Thou art my beloved Son, in whom I am well pleased. And immediately the Spirit driveth him into the wilderness. And he was there in the wilderness forty days, tempted of Satan; and was with the wild beasts; and the angels ministered unto him."

If we say this is poetry, we're not saying it's

unhistorical, but simply that a bare record of outward events can't convey the truth about man, and so the truth about the Son of Man.

What does the story tell us?

Notice first that it is by the Spirit that Jesus is driven, thrown out is the actual word, into the wilderness, the same Spirit which had brought him the conviction of being called to do great things. The Spirit is ourselves in the depths of what we are. It is me at the profoundest level of my being, the level at which I can no longer distinguish between what is myself and what is greater than me. So, theologically, the Spirit is called God in me. And it is from this place where God and me mingle indistinguishably that I am thrown out into the wilderness. The story of Jesus reminds us that being thrown out in this way must be an inevitable concomitant of our call to God's service. To feel isolated, to be incapable for the time being of establishing communion, is part of our training. That is because so far our communion has been shallow, mere pirouetting on the surface. We've come to see its superficiality, its unrealness. Hence the feeling of loss. The training doesn't last for ever. In fact, new powers of communion with our world are being built up within us. We are being made the sort of people of whom it can be said, "All things are yours." But it belongs to the training to feel it will last for ever.

And so, we are tempted of Satan. Tempted to give up, to despair. Tempted to cynicism. Tempted sometimes to cruelty. Tempted not to help others when we know we can, because, we think, what's the use? Tempted to banish from our life all that we really hold most dear, and that is love, tempted to lock ourselves up, so that when we pass by people feel, "There goes a dead man." And behind each and all of these temptations is the temptation to disbelieve in what we are, the temptation to distrust ourselves, to deny that it is the Spirit himself which beareth witness with our spirit, God in us. The water in the bucket of my soul doesn't look like the ocean. Yet every Sunday we affirm that it is. For in the creed at the Holy Communion we speak of the Spirit as he who with the Father and the Son together is worshipped and glorified. We say it, but every day we're tempted not to believe it. And this self-distrust conjures up the wild beasts. Sometimes they're sheer terror, panic, which makes us feel about the most ordinary undangerous things, "I can't do it." Or the wild beasts are the violent rages roaring inside us, triggered off by something ridiculously insignificant – a word, a glance, a failure to show interest in some petty concern. Or the beasts prowl around snarling as envy, hatred, malice, and all uncharitableness.

This then is our Lent, our going with Jesus into the wilderness to be tempted. And we might apply to it some words from the First Epistle of St Peter: "Beloved, do not be surprised at the fiery ordeal which comes upon you to prove you, as though something strange were happening to you. But rejoice, in so far as you share Christ's sufferings, that you may also rejoice and be glad when his glory is revealed."

Christ's glory is his full and satisfying communion with all that is. It is the opposite of being isolated. All things are his and he fills all things. This complete communion springs from a love which is able to give to the uttermost, a love which doesn't give in order to get, but which finds in the act of giving itself its own perfect satisfaction. To love is to give. To give is to be. To be is to find yourself in communion with all about you. And this communion is glory. Christ's glory and yours. You don't have to wait for it until you die or the world comes to an end. It can be yours now.

Accept your wilderness. From the story of the Son of Man realize what your Lent really means, and then the angels will minister to you as they did to him. In other words, you'll find moments when giving for love's sake really satisfies you, really makes you feel alive and in contact. And at such moments Christ's glory is revealed, and we rejoice and are glad. We look at the travail of our soul and are satisfied. Lent, we discover, is Easter in disguise.

Gethsemane

We heard in the lesson this evening St Matthew's account of Jesus in the Garden of Gethsemane. Christians have always believed that Jesus was truly and fully man. He wasn't a god dressed up in the body of a man as though manhood were a suit of clothes. According to St Paul, Jesus emptied himself of his Godhead. Whatever this means, it means that his experience as a human being was identical with our own. He did not know everything in the past and future. He knew just as much and just as little as we do. Nor, having emptied himself of his Godhead, could he restore it to himself as an emergency measure. He had no more power in reserve than the ordinary human person. As the New Testament says, he was in all things like unto us.

In the light of these facts, what happened to Jesus in the Garden of Gethsemane? He was frightened, indeed St Mark says he was panic-stricken. Why? For a variety of reasons. First of all, he was cornered. Any sane man in his position would have known that he could no longer escape the authorities and that the authorities would execute him. And what had happened to his life-work, his mission? It lay in ruins. One of the twelve disciples had already betrayed

him. The others, he could see, were, like himself, perplexed, and could not take much more. They would desert
him soon. To the three of them he knew best, he opened
something of his heart, trying to tell them a little of what he
was going through so that they could share it with him and
support him with their understanding. But it was too much
for them. They could not take it in. They were stupefied.
And when he turned to them for reassurance they had
found escape from his trouble in sleep. Jesus was left
entirely alone with his panic and horror.

Even we ourselves in a small way know something of
what it is like to be cornered and up against what has become
out of our control, how we go over things in our mind, go
over and over them again. This will help us to understand a
little of what Jesus was thinking in Gethsemane. Had he
done the right thing in attacking the authorities so aggressively? If they were now set on killing him, was not that
chiefly his own fault? If he had been more restrained,
quieter and more tactful, the authorities would not now be
seeking his blood. He might still be teaching the crowds,
largely unopposed. And wouldn't that have been better for
everybody concerned? Had he not perhaps been too hasty,
too violent? Going into the temple and driving out the
money-changers and traders with whips – wasn't that suici-
dally provocative? And if he had been overemphatic and in
too much of a hurry, perhaps that showed that somewhere
he wasn't certain of himself. When he was baptized in the
Jordan and struggled with temptation in the wilderness, he
had felt supremely confident that he was right. And when
the crowds came to listen to his teaching and the sick people
he touched were healed, there seemed no shadow of a doubt
that he was God's Messiah. But now? The old confidence,
the old certainty, had left him.

Perhaps from the start he had been the victim of an illusion. After all, that sort of thing had occurred fairly frequently in the history of his people. They had always had their false prophets as well as their true ones. And many of the false prophets had been sincere enough according to their lights. They had just been a bit mad, that was all. Had he been a bit mad too? And was this the moment of disillusioning sanity? Had he sacrificed everything to a fanatic's dream? After all, his relatives had thought him mad, and at one point had tried to force him to come home. And how ruthless he had been with them for the sake of the cause he thought he embodied. He had disowned them when they came to look for him – his mother, his sisters and brothers, all of them – and he had said that his real mother and sisters and brothers were those who followed him. Wasn't that to get things out of proportion, evidence perhaps of an insane conceit?

Perhaps Judas Iscariot was right and it was best for everybody that he should be arrested and crucified. And Judas, what right had he to bring untold suffering and calamity upon the head of Judas? For that was certain to happen. Judas had a great deal of loyalty in him, a great deal of good. That is why he had chosen Judas to be a special friend. Had he not stretched Judas's loyalty and love, all those good qualities which had made him so obvious a choice, stretched them beyond all human endurance? And so, was not he himself responsible for his own betrayal by Judas? Judas would feel intolerable remorse, that was certain, and it would lead him to do something desperate. And was not he himself to blame, even more, much more, than Judas?

No wonder Peter, James and John were asleep. He had rebuked them, and talked of watching and praying, but what right had he to demand sympathy on so colossal a scale? Wasn't it best for them that they couldn't give it? Let them sleep on and take their rest. The doubt, the insufferable turmoil, the going over of things in his mind again and again, the agony, were his and his alone. There was nobody to share his desperate uncertainty, the torturing doubts, the terrifying emptiness, the menace from outside of his approaching arrest and execution, and the infinitely worse menace from inside of disillusion and despair.

So it was that Jesus prayed, "Father, if it be possible, let this cup pass from me." He was human enough to want to be let off what he was going through, humble and honest enough to admit it. But the simple request from the depths of the heart, "Let this cup pass from me", was qualified: "Father, if it be possible." It is natural and absolutely right that we should not wish to be put too severely to the test. But, having said this, we must add that God is most emphatically not an escape from human ills enabling us to evade the horrors and suffering of human life. Too often in the past, God and religion have been presented as painkillers, as though God were a magician who will melt our troubles away like snow in the sun, giving us a divine relief from the hard facts of the real world. But God is not a funkhole, however much Christians may have tried to use him as one. And this is what Jesus understood when to his natural request for relief he added, "If it be possible."

It was not possible. What menaced Jesus from outside and tortured him from within could not be removed. The betrayer came with the police, the friends of Jesus deserted him and ran away in a panic. He was duly arrested, sentenced and executed. Nor, as far as we can tell from our earliest record, St Mark, did Jesus find peace or the quiet of certainty. For most of the time he was silent and had nothing to say. At the end, just before he died, he cried out, "My God, My God, why has thou forsaken me?"

As with Jesus, so with us, there is no escape from the human situations in which we find ourselves. God will not say, "Abracadabra", and get us out of it. Nor will he supply us with a spiritual drug to deaden whatever doubt or anxiety or fear or pain may come our way, and cheer us up so that we feel good. Perhaps we confuse escape with something quite different: victory. For Jesus there was no escape. But there was victory. Yet how, if he died deserted by men and feeling forsaken by God? How victory?

The victory consisted precisely in not running away, in not trying to escape. In things outside this meant staying in Jerusalem and facing the worst his enemies could do. That is obvious. More important, it meant squarely facing the enemies inside — the doubts, the despair, the perplexity, the panic, the isolation. From these enemies inside, Jesus did not hide under a cloak of illusion, pretending to himself that things were better than they were and that he was feeling like a hero. He accepted his agony — not a glorious uplifting experience, but an experience powerful to wound and warp and destroy. He accepted what he thus found within him. He knew that there would be no angels to bear him up and guard him from all ills.

And by thus facing and accepting what came to him from outside and from within, without lessening the agony, he mastered it. He made it into his servant. He used it as the way of surrender, of giving all. The agony of which he might have been no more than the victim was by acceptance converted into the instrument of his will. He had always wanted to give himself. And when, as now, he was stripped of everything and had nothing to give, by consenting to receive that state of affairs and not hiding away from it, he used it to give himself totally. That was his victory. That is how he mastered what happened to him. We shall be celebrating the victory on Easter Day, but it is present already in Gethsemane. Easter turns the light on a situation already present and shows it in its true colours for what it really is. If Jesus was victorious, it was on this night before he died.

And what of us? It is unlikely that we shall ever have to go through an experience as deep and devastating as Christ's own in Gethsemane. But we may sometime approach it, even if only from afar. Somebody we love and on whom we depend may die. Or our material circumstances may unexpectedly change for the worse. Or something we had set our heart on and were working for devotedly may collapse into nothing. Or perhaps already we have discovered that our real enemies are inside us, that we have an unfortunate temperament in this way or that, that we are assertive or quarrelsome or timid or prone to worry and be anxious, vaguely but disturbingly frightened of something — we don't quite know what. Or perhaps we shall be ploughed up, turned inside out by a turbulent, unsatisfied love. If any of these things are true of us, or become true — and examples could be multiplied *ad infinitum* — then God won't provide a magic escape. If we look to him to do that, we shall feel he has let us down.

What God will enable us to do is to face these unpleasant, ugly, disturbing, frightening, something agonizing facts or feelings. To face them without dodging or pretending to ourselves that things are different, and thus to accept them. "This is me." "This is the corner I am in." "This is how I feel." And as with Jesus, so with us, the acceptance will bring the victory. By not evading our circumstances, outside us and inside, we shall cease to be their victim and make them bring us the very life which they would rob us of.

I know a man who was blinded in the war. He was invalided out of the army. Life seemed at an end for him. At first he bitterly resented what had happened to him. For a time, his inner turmoil, his anger and hatred and exasperation and despair caused him even more suffering than his blindness. Then gradually he began to accept not only his blindness, but also his immense resentment at it. After about a year, he discovered that he could compose music (although somebody else had to write it down for him). His music has not yet been published. Perhaps it never will be. But that is irrelevant. He wasn't looking for fame or reputation. He was looking for life. And he found it in the music he composes. A few years ago, he said to me, ''You'll think it very odd, but before I was blinded my life was terribly shallow. I sometimes wonder whether I was alive at all. Now I have found a richness and peace which before were unimaginable. Of course, being blind is still hell. But I have learnt to live with it and the privations it brings. And had I not been blinded, I don't think I should ever have discovered the deep happiness I now possess underneath the pain.'' This man had been with Jesus in Gethsemane. He had mastered his fate by accepting it.

When that happens, we want to thank God, because the evil, which is real and hurts, the evil from which we suffer, is changed, transfigured, into good. The very evil which destroys brings us life and peace and joy. Jesus spoke of his passion and death, all the agony of it, as the cup he had to drink. He gives this cup to us to drink with him. This means pain, and to drink the cup is to accept the pain. But then we find that the cup is something else as well, which is more important and final: the cup of blessing which is the communion of the blood of Christ. As the hymn puts it,

> *And oh what transport of delight*
> *From thy pure chalice floweth*.

Cross

People who study dreams scientifically tell us that each of the characters we dream about is really us – aspects of us we refuse normally to meet, but which we are willing to meet when they come disguised as "somebody else". The dream doesn't tell us anything unless we can see through the disguise.

So it is with the historical event of the cross. Unless we see it as *our* story and not merely a story about other people, it will reveal nothing to us. And certainly this is how the first Christians regarded it. Think, for instance, of the language St Paul uses. He speaks of suffering with Christ, of being crucified with Christ, of dying with him, of being buried with him, of being raised from the dead and exalted with him. And St Paul didn't think of this as some private, esoteric, mystical experience of his own, unattainable by people of lesser spiritual capacity than himself, but as the common lot of all Christian believers. "Do you not know," he asks in some surprise of the Christians in Rome – "do you not know that all of us who have been baptized into Christ Jesus were baptized into his death? We were buried, therefore, with him by baptism into death, so that as Christ was raised from the dead by the glory of the Father, we too might walk in newness of life."

The apostle went further than this. In Christ crucified, he said, we can even find the clue to everything that is, the ultimate explanation of all things. For "in him all things were created, in heaven and on earth," and "in him all things hold together." The cross of Christ here reaches out to grasp the entire universe. That's why we cannot regard Holy Week as merely referring back to a number of past events, however important. It's more like a detailed model of what it means to be a human being, an analysis of the atmosphere in which we live and move, something never past but always round us, engulfing us, like the air we breathe.

While this world lasts the cross is always contemporary. To treat the cross as no more than a past event, or the resuscitation of a past event, is to evade it.

The final wonder of the cross, it always seems to me, is not the death of Jesus in physical agony. Many men have died in torture. It is that Jesus appears to have had that terrible destroying sense of being out of joint with everything, what we have described as the feeling of non-relation, the feeling of being shut up in the prison-house of your own self, mean, ugly, incapable of loving, and so, unlovable. I do not see how else we are to understand his cry, "My God, my God, why hast thou forsaken me?" It is the cry of a person who feels he is in a hell of isolation. And it means that when we feel something of this sort, we are no longer locked up in our own agonizingly individual private world, but sharing in an experience which God himself has undergone. In order to show us the depth of his love and thereby to establish personal contact with us, in Christ crucified, God himself felt love ruled out as a possibility. He felt unable to love and so, unlovable. When you consider that God's very nature is love, that the giving and receiving of love constitutes his eternal beatitude, here you can just begin to apprehend the cost to him of this experience. God cared enough for us even for that.

What, therefore, the cross of Christ demonstrates to us is that, in spite of all evidence to the contrary both outside us and within us, reality is not hostile to us but absolutely on our side, ready to stand by us and take our part at whatever cost. This produces confidence, and it is on the basis of this confidence that we are ready to establish communion with our world. If we are the sons of God's love, then we need not be frightened of what we are. We can welcome ourselves as we would welcome a trusted friend. And the more I am thus in personal relation to everything I am, the more shall I be able to afford communion with other people. Since I no longer despise myself, I shall no longer have to fear their adverse opinion of me. If given, it will no longer echo and authenticate what I myself feel, and hence its sting will be drawn. I shall then be free to give myself away. And in this giving, I shall possess all things.

In the light of the Easter faith, we know Jesus to have given his life for the greatest of all causes, the salvation of mankind. But this does not appear to be what he felt in Gethsemane – "Horror and dismay came over him, and he said to them, 'My heart is ready to break with grief; stop here, and stay awake' " – nor upon the cross when he cried aloud "My God, my God, why hast thou forsaken me?"

It is possible that we may be given a glimpse of the inner reality of his passion if we consider it as a total loss on his part of all sense of his own value due to his oneness with mankind in its inward conflicts. When such loss occurs, it is natural to look for consolation from friends. But a Peter, a James, and a John cannot supply from without what has been taken away from within. They cannot but be asleep to the agonizing need, however genuine their goodwill. And, meanwhile, when there is a total loss of the sense of one's own value, there emerge, as an attempt at distraction, blind hatred and rage, all the worse for their having no consistent target. And then follows despair, not as a passive state of quiescence, but as something which hurls itself against a brick wall and cries aloud to the empty air. If this is a possible and legitimate way of approaching the mystery of Christ's passion, it shows us something of the meaning of the atonement he wrought. It does not speak of crimes and judges and punishments and acquittals. It speaks indeed of justice. For "He [God] made us; He maintained us in our pain. At least, however, on the Christian showing, He consented to be Himself subject to it. If, obscurely, He would not cease to preserve us in the full horror of existence, at least He shared it. He became as helpless as we under the will which is He. This is the first approach to a sense of justice in the whole situation."*

But it speaks of more than justice. It speaks of change and transfiguration. Christ's total loss of the sense of his own value, which is ten thousand times worse than physical pain or death, was the stuff and substance which God raised up in glory. In Christ, God made it into the material of a full and infinitely satisfying communion with all that is. In Christ, God took inward agony and rage and torture, and made of them eternal life which is eternal love. It is thus perhaps that we may consider the atonement he wrought in the death and resurrection of his Son. When we ourselves suffer these things, it is with Christ we suffer them. And because this is so, although the pain continues, we know it also as the glory of God.

* Charles Williams, *Selected Writings* (Oxford University Press, 1961), chosen by Anne Ridler, pp. 95–96.

Who then devised the torment? Love.
Love is the unfamiliar Name
Behind the hands that wove
The intolerable shirt of flame
Which human power cannot remove. *

In Christ God converted the destructive fire of our human agony into the living and life-giving flame which is himself. The former contributes to and is made part of the latter. So the agony itself can now be seen in its change and transfiguration as the gift of his love. It is not therefore a surprise that many of the saints displayed symptoms of a psychopathological kind. St Paul's sudden blindness on the road to Damascus was the physical consequence of a profound psychic disturbance. It was one of the ways in which, for a period, he bore on his body the marks of Jesus.

And when they were come to the
place, which is called Calvary, there
they crucified him . . . Then said
Jesus, Father, forgive them; for they
know not what they do.
St Luke 23:33 and 34.

We can begin to understand how Jesus's word of forgiveness works out in our own lives only if we recognize that we have, all of us, been injured in some way or other. We are all of us, in some sense or other, damaged goods. We all of us have a history in which the forces of destruction have

* T. S. Eliot, *Little Gidding,* iv.

played their part. To some of us it has shown itself in some obvious catastrophe – somebody we loved has died, or we have been maimed by an accident or illness, or our affections have been deeply wounded. But over and above these obvious catastrophes there remain for all of us the unknown injuries hidden in the depths of what we are and which manifest themselves only as things like boredom or irritation or discontent or resentment or deadness or despair – the things which prompt us to hit out as we do.

We must forgive ourselves for being, inevitably, damaged goods. We must look at our damaged selves with compassion and acceptance just as we would so look at a man screaming because he was in extreme physical agony. To forgive and accept our damaged selves is to realize that we are much more than the damage, that we are also people attractively alive and lovable and precious. And if we ask what right we have thus to forgive and accept ourselves, the answer is that God has already forgiven and accepted us and that is what the cross is about. "Father, forgive them for they know not what they do."

This kind of forgiveness won't be accomplished all in a moment. We shall have slowly to grow in the forgiveness of ourselves, and the growth will be God calling us into being by his creative love, until we know beyond a peradventure that his words are fully true of us, fully true of me: "Thou art my beloved son in whom I am well pleased."

To the degree in which we forgive and accept ourselves because God has already forgiven and accepted us so that now in this present time we are his sons, to that degree shall we be able to forgive others, to forgive the people who have really injured us. To forgive an injury is not to condone it, to pretend it doesn't matter. We shall face the injury squarely, recognizing its destructive power and the pain it has inflicted on us. But as we know ourselves as infinitely more than the person injured, so we shall also know the offender as infinitely more than the person who did the injury; for he acted, partly at least, under hidden compulsions, not knowing what he did. And when he sees that we recognize him as so much more than the damaged goods who did the injury, Christ's creative word will flow out through us to him and his own true self will begin to live and grow.

People in the end behave as they are treated. They assume the role for which they are cast by society. Suppose, for instance, that when Jesus saw Zaccheus in the tree he had said (with perfect truth as far as it went): "You dirty scoundrel, swindler and thief, how dare you show your face in public?" But Jesus didn't. He said, "Zaccheus, hurry up and come down because I want you to give me lunch." So was the real Zaccheus created, the Zaccheus who for the sheer joy of it hurried away to give away half his goods. But that, of course, was an exceptional case. Our acceptance of others may sometimes bring those quick results. But very seldom indeed. More often our acceptance and forgiveness of others will be a slow and costly process in the course of which we shall be rebuffed and kicked about and hurt. One thing for certain does nothing but harm, and that is when we are starry-eyed about others and allow cheap, easy, nice feelings about them to blind us to what they really are. Because people, all of us, behave destructively, it shows that destructiveness is a real and very powerful element in our make-up. The last thing we must do is to ignore it and pretend to ourselves that there is a cheap and easy way by which we can be changed.

Jesus, we are told, knew what was in man. He knew the strength of man's destructive potential. And therefore he also knew, he more than guessed, that to change people, to create them anew by forgiveness and acceptance, would lead him, as it did, to suffering and death. And to share some at least of his weariness and pain, to share something of his cross, is the price we may well have to pay in order to share in his creative work of forgiveness.

When I recognize and confront the destructiveness within myself, when I accept and receive it as mine, with all the attendant discomfort and agony, all the seething turmoil, or all the deadness and despair, then I am absorbing and rendering harmless that particular degree of destructiveness I feel and I am, sharing with Jesus in his mighty work of bearing the sin of the world, and thus taking it away. And I can help thus to take it away only to the degree in which I am willing to feel its awful power in me.

So don't let us ever be frightened to cry with Jesus: "My God, my God, why hast thou forsaken me?" Or perhaps we shall put it in our own words, often in strong and sometimes in what to the undiscerning may seem blasphemous language.

It is not without significance that Jesus's cry of real agony was understood to echo a particular psalm. For the psalm echoed speaks of the triumph of goodness, of peace, and joy and love and life precisely through and by means of the agony and turmoil and despair of God's servant. That is what Jesus did for us upon the cross, and he calls us to be fellow-workers with him. And when we thus suffer with him, we can be sure of this — even now we are being raised with him to newness of life, that newness of life which is for all mankind. The road to the power of Christ's resurrection goes through the cry, "My God, why hast thou forsaken me?" It is by means of our experience of chaos and destruction – the noise of passions ringing us for dead unto a place where is no rest – it is along that road that Christ's promise to us is being fulfilled: "Behold, I make all things new." In sharing Christ's conflict, we inevitably also share his victory.

And when Jesus had cried with a loud
voice, he said, Father, into thy hands I
commend my spirit: and having said
thus, he gave up the ghost.
St Luke 23:46

It is, I suppose, good for us to be told that a great deal depends upon what we do or fail to do. But there is a very much more important truth, the ultimate truth that in the end all we can do is to hand over, to commend ourselves and other people and the world into God's hands, because by means of everything which happens God is ceaselessly working out his unfailing purposes of love. The advice which we are often given is to keep going. But God finally revealed himself and performed the last and greatest of his mighty works by means of a man who couldn't keep going at all because he was dying. Instead of keeping going, Jesus commended his spirit into his Father's hands, handing over into God's safe keeping everything he was, everything he had done or failed to do. His last word upon the cross was a word of faith, of trustfulness.

It is hard for us to see properly the depth and extent of this faith and trustfulness because we see Jesus upon the cross with the benefit of hindsight, in the light of the resurrection, of Pentecost, of the triumphant spread of the gospel throughout the Roman world, of two thousand years of Christian history. But when Jesus was actually dying all that was in the unknown future. The present spoke only of failure – the collapse of Jesus's life-work summed up in the flight of the only followers he had left. Yet, as man, Jesus knew that in the last analysis this didn't matter, that nothing mattered except the fact that behind all appearances God was in control accomplishing his work for the world. So Jesus gathered together all his hopes and fears and aspirations and disappointments into this one act of faith – "Father, into thy hands I commend my spirit". And it was by this committal of everything to God in trustfulness that the powers of destruction were conquered by God's own creative love.

The mistake which we almost always make is to think that faith is possible only when we feel holy in some way or other, when we are feeling resigned, submissive, meek, when we are inwardly full of some vision of things, or when we are calm inside. Then, we think, and only then, can we say – "Father, into thy hands". But the real true context of that prayer is, as the gospel says, Jesus crying with a loud voice, and crying with a loud voice does not indicate calm, victorious serenity. It indicates the thick of the raging battle. It is when we are being knocked for six here, there and everywhere; when we are feeling the very reverse of holy; when our hatred and resentment seem more than we can bear; when we are in the depths of depression; when life appears utterly meaningless; when we seem to have nothing to live for; when we are just one ghastly, muddled, senseless civil war – it is from the depths of that utter bloodiness that we can and must say, "Father, into thy hands I commend my spirit".

When things are going well or are what we call success-ful, it is not so difficult to believe that God is working his purpose out and that we fit in as part of that purpose. Or when external circumstances are against us, but we have some sort of warm glow inside, some sense of meaning and purpose, some citadel of spiritual certainty, then, too, we can trust that God is achieving something through us. But what requires the greatest faith, the deepest and truest faith, what has sometimes been called naked faith, is when within us, in heart and mind, we find ourselves in the same condition as Jesus upon the cross: we see our life as one untidy pile of unfinished bits and pieces. We have no satisfying sense of achievement. Our spiritual capacities seem blunted, our capacity for joy, for expectation, for love, for life in its many-splendoured variety, for worship, for wonder, for prayer, for God – they all seem dying or dead. It is precisely then that we can have faith, a faith which cannot be rotted or destroyed by external circumstances and which goes much deeper than any warm glow within, a faith which is a desperate leaning on the fact that whatever we have or have not done and however we feel, God's purpose in us and through us is being achieved.

Jesus, as we all know, once spoke of the importance of the widow's mite. God needs that farthing (the farthing which can be said almost not to exist) – God needs that farthing of love, of truth, of fidelity, of courage, from us. And we give it, as the widow did, from our penury, our destitution, our emptiness, from what we are and where we are, from the place where we have been driven by our heredity and environment and our own deliberate choices, probably for the most of us some sort of slum.

The struggle or conflict which our life is ultimately about, the struggle between creativeness and destructiveness, between good and evil, is always in the end a struggle between faith and unbelief. Jesus calls us to share with him not only his conflict but his victory of faith. "Father, into thy hands I commend everything I am and everything I am not." That is the victory which overcomes the world. And it is God's victory in his Son Jesus Christ.

For in our turmoil – our strife and doubt within, our tears and sweat and blood – we are not engaged in an individual, private war, just me and my own damned self. In our turmoil the Son of God himself goes forth to war, and it is by means of our experience of our own and other people's destructiveness that the Son of God is destroying destruction and winning his total cosmic victory for the love which created and continues to create all things. So when, in some form or other, we are going through it rather badly, it is because Christ has put us for the time being with himself in the centre and thick of the battle. And it is precisely here now, in me and in you, that darkness is struggling with light, destruction is struggling with creation, death with life, isolation with communion, unbelief with faith. Those gigantic contraries are fighting it out to a conclusion now in us. And the conclusion is assured. For Christ has been raised from the dead and has won the day finally and for ever for light and creation and life and communion and faith.

So, however bloody we may feel, however desolate, however on edge and at war, we can still make the last earthly prayer of Jesus our own: "Father, into thy hands I commend my spirit". For God is in control. Love reigns victoriously over the universe and we are reigning with him. In the drama of Good Friday and Easter we are shown that that is what life means at its deepest and most real. We shall almost certainly still feel things like malice, fear, emptiness, deadness and the rest. But when we feel them we shall know that we are not their victim, whatever appearances may suggest. For Christ through us is robbing them of their power. And he cannot fail or lose because he has already succeeded and won for all time and for eternity.

God's method of overcoming evil in Christ was not that of crushing it by superior force. That indeed appears to have been one of Our Lord's temptations in the dark night of Gethsemane. "Put up thy sword into its place: for all they that take the sword shall perish with the sword. Or thinkest thou not that I cannot beseech my Father, and he shall even now send me more than twelve legions of angels?" But that was not God's method. "How then should the scriptures be fulfilled, that thus it must be?" No, God's method of overcoming evil was by enduring its fiercest onslaughts up to and including death itself. Jesus submitted himself to the hypocrisy and selfishness of the ecclesiastical authorities, to the cowardice and callousness of the representative of the civil power, to the fickleness and hysteria of the mob, to the legalized brutality of the soldiers. By these things he allowed himself to be nailed to the cross. And there in utter helplessness he died, apparently no longer useful to either God or man – a life poured away and wasted, like the alabaster cruse of exceeding precious ointment which a woman had recently poured upon his head.

If ever evil has seemed to triumph utterly, it was on the evening after Our Lord's crucifixion. The enemies of God, including the last enemy Death, had done their work with consummate efficiency. They had brought Jesus to the dust. He was now a corpse in a tomb. "This", he had said to the armed band which arrested him in the Garden, "is your hour, and the power of darkness."

And yet, in spite of what happened or rather *because* of it, we call that Friday good. For the light shines most brightly exactly where the shadows are blackest. "I, if I be lifted up from the earth, will draw all men unto myself." That was God's method of overcoming evil. That was his way of exercising a power superior to force. And therefore as he died Jesus could say, "It is accomplished". Love's redeeming work was done, and henceforth Christ crucified could be proclaimed to the world as the power and wisdom of God. What looked like the utter defeat of goodness by evil was in reality the final defeat of evil by goodness. What looked like the weakness of a dying man was in reality the strength of the living God. What looked like tragedy was really victory. That is why, as Westcott reminded us, Jesus reigns from the tree. Not because his wounds were less severe than the spectators thought they were, not because his passion was less bitter or terrible than the evangelists have led us to believe, not because his physical weakness was less real or his death, from the human point of view, less catastrophic than the Church has always supposed — but because precisely in and through these things the Son of Man was glorified, since by their means the power of God's love went forth to subdue and capture a rebel world.

Neither the glory nor the power, however, were evident at the time. Then, the whole scene appeared to be occupied by darkness and death. The glory and the power were revealed three days later to the eye of faith when Jesus was raised up from the dead. For his resurrection was no reversal of what had happened previously, as though at the twelfth hour God had set everything right by a *coup de main*. It was rather the lifting up of the cross into the proper realm of truth. It was the manifestation of Calvary for what it really was. It was a proclamation that God's power is made perfect in weakness and that it is through death itself that death is for ever overcome.

If therefore we place upon the cross the figure of Christ crowned and glorified, let us not forget that in so doing we are passing beyond the limits of this world into the infinite area of resurrection-life, to which death was the only door even for the Son of God incarnate. In worshipping the Crucified we worship life, but we must remember that it is Life achieved through and by means of death. "The Christian Gospel", said Oliver Quick, "is a Gospel of life through death, not of a deathless life."

Death and Resurrection

We cannot see the death of Jesus for what it really was – and is – without seeing it, as the first Christians did, in the light of his resurrection. The two belong inseparably together.

From one point of view they are events in the past, things which happened once for all. But what happened once for all to Jesus is happening all the time, happening to us. For in the death and resurrection of Jesus we see a conflict and a victory which are still going on now, a conflict and a victory in which we can see the deepest meaning of our own lives – what our own lives are most truly about.

St Paul talks about Christ reigning until he has put all his enemies under his feet. The drama of Christ's warfare is not yet over. He must reign, said St Paul, until all his enemies are vanquished. We are living in that "until". Final victory is indeed assured. What happened on the first Easter morning can never be undone. But Christ's conflict, his struggle, his warfare, still goes on in us. In us Christ is still being crucified and raised from the dead.

Of what, then, does this conflict and victory consist?

It can take innumerable forms and be put in all sorts of ways. So you will have to supplement what I say from your own experience. But, as I see it, Christ's conflict and victory can be described like this: it is mercy, the mercy which gets spat upon and kicked, victorious over brutality; it is generosity, the generosity which goes on giving, victorious over all that is mean-hearted and close-fisted; it is peace, the peace which entered into hostility and venom, victorious over strife; it is love, the love which made itself vulnerable and suffered, victorious over hatred and cold-heartedness; it is the deep satisfaction of meaning, of purpose fulfilled, victorious over emptiness and despair. And it is in and among ourselves now that mercy struggles with brutality, generosity with meanness, peace with strife, love with hatred and cold-heartedness, meaning and purposefulness with emptiness and despair.

In everything we are and do, we are caught up in this drama of Christ. We are not spectators of his death and resurrection. We are involved in them up to the hilt. In us and among us what is creative is doing battle with what is destructive.

The ultimate human misery consists simply in not being able to love. When the power to love is present, adverse circumstances can still bring immense pain, but the pain is transfigured by the love. Now none of us can love perfectly. And for most of us the capacity to love is limited very severely indeed. And it is the smallness of our capacity to love which makes life flat, stale and unprofitable. You can make your incapacity to love into your Easter offering. For your sake, on the cross, Christ allowed his immense power to love to be taken from him. His loud and exceeding bitter cry shows him as having entered the prison of despair, shut away from loving or feeling loved, in torturing darkness of spiritual death. He invites you to join your unavoidable inability to love to his voluntarily accepted inability. As so joined, it becomes your sacrifice to God. Christ offers it with his own perfect sacrifice. It becomes your share in his death. And if this is what you do with your lovelessness, then be sure that, with Christ, God will raise you from your present deadness by his own creative love. You will be filled with the joy of God's love. And it won't stop with you. Others will perceive it and be kindled at it.

There is nothing of what you are which cannot thus be used to bring the power of Christ's resurrection to bear upon this world. This is Christ's Easter victory, and yours.

It was the manhood of Jesus which was raised up on the first Easter Day, the manhood in which the manifold experiences of his earthly life were present and included. As a sign and guarantee of this fact, his risen body still bore the marks of the nails and of the spear. What happened to him on the cross was not something left behind when he rose from the dead. It was present with him as a permanent possession. He did not, after death, retire into the distant heaven, as though he had made from thence a brief excursion earthwards. The eternity of his risen life included that very manhood which had been developed and matured by his experiences in time. And those experiences were thereby given permanence. That which appeared to be fleeting and ephemeral was now seen to possess an abiding value.

In the risen manhood of Christ, the earthly was exalted into the heavenly, so that the changes and chances of this fleeting world became the very stuff out of which was built the City of God. Time, as that which breaks the unity of life into a thousand unsatisfying fragments and leaves behind the things we love to perish and be forgotten – time in this sense was conquered by the resurrection of Jesus. Its death-dealing sting was finally drawn.

People do well to be sceptical of beliefs not anchored in present experience, for they invariably belong to the land of compensatory dreams. Scepticism, said Santayana, is the chastity of the intellect. And no age perhaps has been more chaste than our own. We may indeed, in the words of W. H. Auden, be in danger of becoming tight-arsed old maids. But that does not mean that we should expect people to throw chastity completely to the winds and indulge in orgies of extravagant rubbish. Fantasies dissociated from daily life must be rejected if we are not to grow mentally and spiritually soft.

At this point I find myself wanting as a Christian to claim that this anchor in daily life is provided by my personal experience here and now of Christ raised from the dead. I say my prayers. I read the Bible. I go to church. I receive the sacraments. And cannot I truly claim that in the course of these activities I have communion now with Christ as a living person?

Most certainly I can. At the same time honesty requires that a number of comments be made.

Reality, to begin with, always comes to us wrapped up in illusion, as Christian writers have been the first to point out. What therefore I consider my experience of Christ raised from the dead cannot be simply or only that. It will also contain projections from my own unconscious wishes and thus be partly a private fantasy. Christians are not exempt from man's habitual tendency to make gods in his own image. There is also another even more important fact which I cannot ignore. Maybe that after a painfully long and perplexing journey I do discover something of the reality of the living Christ. But what I then find is remarkably similar and often identical with what has been found by unwearied seekers who either started as Jews, Buddhists, Vedantists, or Moslems, or who have found this mysterious reality without having hung any religious label round their necks. That indeed is what I should expect if I equate Christ with the Eternal Word which enlighteneth every man. But I find that I and my fellow Christians do not always expect it. On the contrary, I find it often causes suspicion and anxiety. Intellectual guns are often primed and shot in passion to demonstrate that the Eternal Word is the exclusive possession of Christians. And I am left wondering whether this anxiety to prove exclusive possession does not suggest a confusion of the Eternal Word with a cult-idol (for it is idols which need protecting, not God) – a confusion to which, I suspect, the devotees of all religions are liable.

Hence, although I want to offer my experience of Christ in prayer and sacrament as the anchor in the present of my belief in resurrection, I am doubtful whether the argument is wholly legitimate and surmise that this may be tne reason why, as far as most people are concerned, such so-called witness is totally ineffective. The gem of reality is too wrapped up in the coloured paper of illusion. If what in fact I offer to people is to a large extent my own particular cult-idol – even if it is an idol I share with the majority of churchgoers – then it can be no surprise that it means little or nothing to them. For cult-idols are a matter of temperament and inclination, and there is no reason why the cult-idol which attracts me should attract others. They may be immune to its charms just as they may have no eye for painting or no head for figures. Nor will it be much good my delivering myself a lecture on the fatal inadequacy of private opinion and the strength of the collective opinion of the innumerable company of believers, since a similar innumerable company has appreciated painting and enjoyed doing their accounts. ''I am just not one of them'', the rejoinder will be.

What makes me even more certain that our Christian experience of what we call the living Christ is at least partly an attachment to a cult-idol is our evident immunity from the threatening glory of resurrection. If, as Christians are supposed to believe, Christ *is* the resurrection, it is strange that life for us invariably means business as usual, especially the business we transact with ourselves. Christ's *métier* is generally considered to be the preservation of the *status quo*; in individuals a personal psychic *status quo* and in the church an institutional *status quo*, provided that in each case there is a respectable measure of reform, in the individual mostly moral and in the church mostly administrative. There is little sign of the ultimate challenge of Jesus – ''Destroy this temple and in three days I will raise it up.'' Indeed our main concern is to preserve the fabric – what we like to call our own mental and spiritual health, and the well-being of the church.

But then the advantage of idols, as second-Isaiah perceived, is that they cannot do anything. They thus leave us free to continue as before. And if our cult-idol inconveniently called himself the resurrection, we have insulated ourselves against this threat by pushing resurrection safely out of the present into the past and future. Christ was the resurrection and he will be. That is how we have allayed our fears. So we can eat, drink, and be, if not merry, at least reasonably comfortable, even when we call the fare provided God's holy food. And if anything, like a

Panorama programme for instance, suggests that we have died and need resurrection now, we rush to the defence of our cult-idol and its religious clutter as if the Eternal Word could be threatened, even by the BBC. It is a neat trick (all the neater for being unconsciously done) this banishing of resurrection to past and future. It saves us from a lot of reality and delivers us from a great deal of fear. It has, in short, the advantage of safeguarding us from life.

Yet there is another side to the picture. Without this other side we could have no hope. We should remain permanently the slaves of our cult-idol. But in the mercy of God it is always possible for the coloured paper of illusion to be unwrapped enough to reveal the gem of reality it has so far hidden. The Eternal Word can begin to be revealed in the features of the cult-idol. Error can be the mediator of truth. Darkness can be the vehicle of light. And this in itself is an experience of resurrection now, of resurrection and of the death which must precede it. The death in this case is a death to familiar and childish certainties. The resurrection consists in our being raised up to a first and no doubt fleeting glance of unmanageable mystery.

If religions, or at least the great five or six, do not peter out, can it be because they carry within them the possibility of revealing the Eternal Word to those who have ears to hear? And those who do hear cease to make exclusive jingoist claims for the particular illusions which for them have conveyed the reality. More and more they are compelled to acknowledge that the reality can be found along many and various roads and not least by people who follow no established road at all but cut their own path as they go. The way, the truth, and the life lie on the other side beyond the destruction of the temple. That for many is the most painful death they have to die. It was a death which Jesus accepted. He died upon the cross crying, "My God, my God, why hast thou forsaken me?" We cannot tell the full significance of that cry. But at least it must mean that Jesus surrendered his role or identity as the teacher who brought to men good news from God, the man certain of his vocation as messiah, the figure in whom God's truth was ultimately revealed. In that loud and exceeding bitter cry such claims and certainties were cast aside and given up in a death which preceded the moment of his dying physically. And it was because of this renunciation that he was given a name which is above every name. "Destroy this temple" — the temple was himself and all he was, his beliefs, his hopes, his certainties, his identity as the one sent from the Father. But if the temple was destroyed, it was only that it might be raised indestructible. It was in the surrender of all he was that he became transparent to the Eternal Word in whom all things in heaven and on earth are to be gathered into one.

In the surrender of the cross Jesus is shown to be the opposite of a cult-idol. Cult-idols are neurotically concerned to preserve each its own exclusive rights, "for they that make them are like unto them". Jesus abandons all his claims in the stripping naked of Calvary. And it is precisely because of his nakedness that he is able to reveal the Eternal Word. For the Eternal Word is not in competition with other claimants. He is not in this sense a successful Pretender. And so he can make himself heard in all languages by all races, and his voice can come to be recognized speaking by means of all religions or none.

But how, then, can we know that we have heard the Eternal Word?

It is by the fact that to hear him is always to be raised from the dead. Where there is resurrection, there the Eternal Word has spoken. And where there is no resurrection, there the voice of the Eternal Word has not yet penetrated, be men never so earnest, be they never so religious.

But what, then, is resurrection? If it happens to us now, how are we to identify it? How are we to know that it has occurred or is occurring? What are the signs of its coming?

What we hanker after is a sign from heaven which cannot be spoken against, an experience in which we are lifted out of the tears and sweat and dirt of our humanity into a serene empyrean where the gritty quality of our ordinary daily life is left far behind and can be forgotten. But resurrection as a present miracle does not deliver us from the unevenness and turmoil and fragmentariness of being human. The miracle is to be found precisely within the ordinary round and daily routine of our lives. Resurrection occurs to us as we are, and its coming is generally quiet and unobtrusive and we may hardly be aware of its creative power. It is often only later that we realize that in some way or other we have been raised to newness of life, and so have heard the voice of the Eternal Word.

To give some concrete examples.

An artist, at first only painfully aware of an utter emptiness and impotence, finds his imagination gradually stirred into life and discovers a vision which takes control of him and which he feels not only able but compelled to express. That is resurrection. Or a scholar or scientist as he pursues his research finds a favourite theory breaking up in his hands. He is left with no home in which to house the quantities of evidence he has collected. Then a new more adequate theory gradually takes shape in his mind which makes him more at home with his material even than he was before. That is resurrection. Or a married couple find their old relationship, once rich and fulfilling, slowly drying up into no more than an external observance to the point where it seemed impossible that these dry bones should ever live again. Then a new relationship emerges, less superficially high powered and less greedy than the old one, but deeper, more stable, more satisfying, with a new quality of life which is inexhaustible because it does not depend on the constant recharging of emotional batteries. That is resurrection.

Or an individual finds life less and less rewarding, not on its public and professional side, where he may be very successful, but in its failing to bring in an adequate degree of personal fulfilment. He seems to get less and less of what he wants and values most, although he does not know what it is. He feels intolerably isolated on a rubbish dump he cannot get off. He has identified what he is with a limited and false portrait of himself which he was successfully sold by an unconscious conviction that limitation means safety. But the supposed claims of safety are emptying his life of content. Yet in the midst of his despair he discovers a broader basis on which to establish himself, and, in spite of the threatening danger, fills up more of his own space, lets himself in for more of what he is, and thus finds a richer more satisfying life. That is resurrection.

Or suffering, a severe illness, or a catastrophe like the premature death of someone deeply loved, such suffering is always destructive. People, we say, are never the same again. Sometimes they shrivel up and atrophy. But appearances here can be deceptive. Under the devastation of their ordeal which leaves its deep and permanent traces, one can be aware that they are in touch with a new dimension of reality. They have somehow penetrated to the centre of the universe. They are greater people. They are more deeply alive. That is resurrection.

Or, on a lighter but by no means insignificant level, the prisoner of irritating or confining circumstances, the man who slips on one of the many kinds of banana skin, the man whose great expectations are belied, the man who is tied to triviality, realizes the humour of his situation, and by his laughter shows that he has risen above what cabins and confines him because he can relish the joke at his own expense. That is resurrection.

Resurrection is always a mystery. It is always a miracle. It is always the creative act of the Eternal Word. Because that Word is spoken now in the present in terms of what we call the common circumstances of life, there can be nobody who at some time or other has not thus been raised from the dead. But more often than not our eyes are holden and we do not know it. We do not recognize resurrection when it comes to us. The presence of the eternal Word is unnoticed, and evidenced only in the new life made available; just as at Cana of Galilee the guests enjoyed the good wine but did not know whence it was.

If we have been aware of resurrection in this life, then, and only then, shall we be able or ready to receive the hope of final resurrection after physical death. Resurrection as our final and ultimate future can be known only by those who perceive resurrection with us now encompassing all we are and do. For only then will it be recognized as a country we have already entered and in whose light and warmth we have already lived.

3
Affirmations

Prayer

Simplicity in prayer – childlike trust in God – our part
and God's – of distractions, difficulties and the
presence of God – being honest before God – if you
want to blaspheme . . . – the communion of saints
and the consequences of our interrelatedness – seeing
things as God sees them – the effects of prayer.

I have come to the conclusion that when all is said and done, the only real prayer I can say is that of the blind beggar in the gospels, "Lord Jesus, that I may receive my sight". Let me see the real root cause of that spiritual sophistication which separates me from God. Let me see God's real presence encompassing me, enfolding me, always everywhere. Let me see that wherever I am or whatever I am doing, whether I feel tired or excited, angry or amused, a success or a failure, fed up or enthusiastic, a bundle of nerves or calm and quiet, miserable or happy, optimistic or in despair, whatever it may be, let me see that all I have to do is to turn simply to God and say, "Hello, it is me."

There is no need to stand on ceremony because I am at home in my Father's house. And there is no need to keep up appearances by pretending that I am a worse person than I am, or even a better person, because God knows what I am like infinitely better than I do myself. "Hello, it is me, your old friend and your old enemy, your loving friend who often neglects you, your complicated friend, your utterly perplexed and decidedly resentful friend, partly loving, partly hating, partly not caring. It is me." When in your heart you even half say that (which means you half don't say it) maybe in a queue waiting for a bus which doesn't come, then there is joy in heaven among the angels of God.

God is leading us towards simplicity, to childlike trust in him and love for him by his freely given grace which is his own divine presence at work within us. And his grace works not in spite of what we are but by means of what we are. In other words, we draw near to simplicity to the degree in which we become our full true selves.

Our job is to put ourselves at God's disposal by the discipline of regularity, by faithfulness to our rule, and by the use of that common sense without which we can't do anything. But there our job ends. What happens when we pray is God's business, not ours. God will give us what he knows is best. And what is best we see in the life of Jesus, in his joy and peace and stillness and confidence and trust. And also in his passion, his bloody sweat, his death and resurrection.

We shall often be besieged by wandering and irrelevant thoughts. When that happens we must remember that we are much more than the thoughts which wander. While on the surface of our mind we are reminding ourselves that we must collect a suit from the cleaners or wondering whether Mrs Smith enjoyed the concert last night, we may be in active communion with God on a deeper level of our mind. So when our thoughts wander it doesn't mean that all we are is wandering. I am quite sure that trying desperately to concentrate on the superficial level of the mind is a mistake. We must just recall that superficial level to where we really and profoundly are, even if we have to recall it a dozen times a minute.

But when we try this kind of prayer we can be besieged not only by wandering irrelevant thoughts but also sometimes by feelings of savage hatred against somebody or resentment: some smouldering anger, some corrosive anxiety, some deadening sense of depression. If we find ourselves in that sort of state we can say: "Oh God, I am hellishly angry; I think so and so is a swine; I am tortured by worry about this or that; I am pretty certain that I have missed my chances in life; this or that has left me feeling terribly depressed. But nonetheless here I am like this, feeling both bloody and bloodyminded, and I am going to stay here for ten minutes and use my book.* You are most unlikely to give me anything. I know that. But I am going to stay for the ten minutes none the less.'' If you can say something like that, it shows how very near to God you in fact are in spite of your feelings. Or perhaps better, not in spite of your feelings but because of them.

But how can you be close to God because you are feeling angry or resentful or worried or depressed? Well, the New Testament often speaks of Christ's sufferings, his passion, death and resurrection as a conflict and a victory. Christ in his passion is in conflict with all the destructive forces in the world, and by his passion he overcomes destructiveness and wins the day for creativeness. That is what his resurrection shows forth, the victory of creative love over everything that destroys. Christ sometimes invites us, especially when we pray, (though not only when we pray) to share his conflict with him. Our feelings of anger, worry, depression or whatever, are signs that for the time being Christ is calling us to stand with him in the thick of the battle, to face within us the forces of destruction. And since it is with Christ that we are standing in the thick of the battle, then although we will probably continue to feel bloody and bloodyminded, in deepest reality Christ's victory over destructiveness will be working itself out within us and by means of us. That is what St Paul meant when he said that in the degree in which we share the fellowship of Christ's sufferings, to that degree we are also partakers of the power of his resurrection.

So if on occasion you have not so much a boring as a bad time when you pray, with the noise of passions apparently ringing you for dead unto a place where is no rest, then remember what is really happening. It is Christ

* The prayer of meditation and contemplation requires some simple discipline, perhaps initially the setting aside of ten minutes twice a week to read and think over a pre-selected passage in the Bible or some other book.

within you feeling the onslaughts of destructiveness and thereby winning the day for his own creative love. By your bad time at prayer you are being the agent of Christ's restoring, saving love. And not just for yourself but for mankind. For in the invisible world we are all most deeply interconnected. No man is an island. No man can live for himself alone or die for himself alone or suffer for himself alone. What happens to us when we pray is happening for all men everywhere.

But of course, our time at prayer won't always be boring or bad. Often we shall be aware of the peace of God, of his majesty and his mercy, of his warm intimate love for us and of his glory. Sometimes it will be as if we were in a small boat gently floating down a stream. If that happens, then don't use the oars any more. In other words, don't stick to the passage of the book you have chosen. Don't go on thinking it out. The book has done its work. By means of it you have rowed yourself out into the middle of the stream, and the stream itself will now take you along. You can rest as you float on, rest in the presence of God and enjoy the stillness of eternity without any more internal chattering. You haven't got to get anywhere, because you are already there. "Be still and know that I am God" – that will have become true of you. Sometimes you will have to row, think over the passage of the book. Sometimes you will find that you can abandon yourself straightaway to the stream.

There is no doubt that the New Testament teaches us to ask God for things. Jesus said "Ask and it shall be given unto you", and St Paul tells us to let our requests be known unto God, while the Epistle of St James tells us bluntly: "You do not have because you do not ask." There is a certain kind of spiritual snobbery which thinks itself above asking God for things. And such snobbery is condemned not only by the passages I have just quoted but also by one of the most sacred moments in all history, when Jesus in the Garden of Gethsemane made *de profundis* the request: "If it be possible let this cup pass from me." So true prayer includes asking for things. There can be no doubt whatever about that.

At the same time we must be very careful to distinguish true prayer from its perverted parody. I am referring to magic. You sometimes hear Christians say "I believe in magic", as though that were a statement of faith and devotion. But if it is, they are misusing the word magic. Magic means manipulating the supernatural, God, to serve your own purposes. "My will be done, O God, and I am going to get you by prayer to do it. I want a certain horse to win the 3.30 and by my prayers I am going to make it win". That is magic. Of course, we seldom express it to ourselves as directly or as crudely as that, but it is often there as a kind of background atmosphere. It is as though we had made a bargain with God in which we undertake something, not necessarily prayer in the literal sense but, shall we say, leading a decent life, on the understanding that God will respond by giving us good luck or at least by preserving us from bad luck. . . .

But if the prayer of petition isn't magic, manipulating God in some way or other to give us what we want, then what is it? I suggest that the prayer of petition is the courage of honesty in the presence of God, the courage before God of being what we are, everything we are without evasion.

Sometimes I shall completely approve of what I really am and think it right. And other times I shan't be too sure. Perhaps in what I want I am being just a bit selfish, perhaps not. At other times again I shall very much disapprove (or at least a part of me will) of what I really am and really want. Let us take each of these in turn.

The doctors, let us say, have diagnosed that I have a kidney complaint but assert that, circumstances being favourable, it can be cured. I am a social worker doing useful work and I want to get back and resume it. Here my petition will be a prayer for complete recovery. And unless I can thus ask God to restore me to health, then God isn't what Jesus said he is: "my Father". My petition here will be the natural request of a child who trusts and loves. And God is inviting me to use my kidney disease as an opportunity to grow in my trust in him and love for him. So without hesitation I can pray "Oh God, make me well".

But take another case: I am not at all rich, but I have a job which is reasonably well paid, and this enables me to keep my wife and family in reasonable comfort. But my job is threatened; maybe I shall be declared redundant. However, I am luckier than most people because a friend of mine has offered me another job if my present job falls through, but this other job is not nearly so well paid. It would cut my salary by half, and the inconvenience and privation which would result are obvious. It would put an awful strain not only upon myself, but upon my family. So, with the courage of honesty in the presence of God, I pray that I may keep my present job. Perhaps I am thinking too much of myself and of my own concerns, perhaps not. Perhaps the question I am really asking myself, and it forms the background of my prayer, is: if I lose my present job, shall I be able to take the consequences of its loss without disintegrating in some way or other? And so I pray "Oh God, let me continue in my present job. Don't let me lose it through redundancy." That prayer is not so very different from the prayer of Jesus in Gethsemane: "Let this cup pass from me." It is only superficially that it sounds selfish. It is really an act of humility. I don't imagine that I am the marvellous sort of person who can take misfortune without being warped or broken. So, like Jesus, I pray for the misfortune not to happen.

But take yet another case. I am an actor with a small part in a theatre in the West End of London. But I am also the understudy of the star. It is rumoured that the star has cancer and will not be able to go on much longer. If he leaves I shall get his part and with it my big chance. Now naturally I want to make my name as an actor and if the star left to go into hospital it would provide me with a superb opportunity. I am a Christian and say my prayers. But what on earth am I to pray for in that situation? If the prayer of petition is being honest in the presence of God without evasion, shouldn't I be sinning against prayer if I simply asked for the star actor (let us call him George) to be kept well for the run of the play? Yet isn't that what, as a Christian, I ought to ask?

I think the answer is that in the prayer of petition I have got to unload my whole heart and mind to God and tell him the whole truth. "O God, I want to be a big success as an actor, so a large and important part of me wants George to succumb to cancer and leave. And that large and important part of me is asking precisely for that. But there is another smaller part of me, at times extremely small, which is generous and wants the best for George, and that smaller part of me is asking you to keep George fit and well. So here I am, coming into your presence with two contra-dictory petitions: let George's cancer develop and keep him well." That is true prayer because it is an expression of my full self and I am not ashamed to admit that it is in a state of civil war. It is no good in prayer pretending to myself and to God that I am only the person who wants George to keep well. God knows better and won't be taken in in the slightest.

God wants us to recognize honestly our full self, and our double contradictory petition will be a sign that we have done precisely that. When, however, we pray, "let George's cancer develop" we may find ourselves adding spontaneously "Christ what a swine I am", and that will mean that our prayer of petition has become a sort of confession: an admission that a large and important part of me needs to be healed and delivered from being a swine. Then we will find that our true prayer has begun to alter, begun to be less contradictory, so that we begin to pray, "O God, make me a great success as an actor, but without allowing any harm to come to George. Keep him well and give me other opportunities." And when that happens, the words of Jesus about Zaccheus will be true of us: "Today has salvation come to this house."

The point I am making is that in the prayer of petition at all costs we must not put on our party clothes and keep up a face saving facade. God can't be taken in, and the only person who is taken in is ourselves. And if we don't face our selfishness and recognize it in our prayers it will be driven underground and appear only in disguise as something noble and good. And selfishness disguised as goodness does the maximum of harm to everybody and especially to ourselves, like that terrible lady who was a good woman in the worst sense of the word.

So shocked are we at the irreverence and so ashamed of the rational absurdity of letting off our aggressions against God, that we repress them so far as God is concerned and appear to ourselves not to feel them. And then we wonder why, after we have prayed so devoutly, we feel so bloody-minded towards poor inoffensive John Smith or sweet little helpful Mary Jones or, more often, the members of our own family. Your wife, you see, has very often to have thrown at her the rotten eggs you really want to throw at God. And the joke is that God is not in the slightest degree taken in by the pantomime by which you deceive yourself. He knows what we won't admit to ourselves, that the rotten eggs are really meant for him.

When we experience God as a meeting with another to whom we are closely linked as to a father or a friend, then the ambivalence of our feelings is inevitable. It is far better to accept that fact honestly and admit it to ourselves than to repress it. There is great wisdom in Mrs Patrick Campbell's warning not to do it in the street and frighten the horses. But that prudent condition observed, if you want to blaspheme, then for Christ's sake blaspheme. If you want in your prayers to grouse, then for Christ's sake grouse. If you hate God, then for Christ's sake tell him you do and tell him why. He will know that these things are the necessary obverse of your love for him and that he is himself responsible for having made you that way. By having the courage of your aggression you will show greater trust in him and greater love for him than by all that "resigned submissive meek" stuff which leaves you to take the hell out of other people, and not least out of yourself so that in consequence there is far less of you to give away.

The real basis of intercession is the fact which, in traditional christian language, is called the communion of saints. We are not isolated entities, each person locked up in himself and impenetrable, individual islands surrounded by seas which nobody can pass over. On the contrary, in the inside of life, in the invisible world, we are all of us, the whole of mankind, closely and deeply interrelated. Our outward contact with each other by sight and hearing and touch is no more than the tip of an iceberg. Outward contact is no more than the visible sign of a far more real, deeper, and closer contact we all have with each other in the most real world there is. St Paul expounded this truth in his teaching about the Body of Christ, and the Body of Christ is potentially mankind as a whole. He says: "If one member suffers, all suffer together, if one member is honoured, all rejoice together." In deepest truth we all belong to one another, we all cohere in each other. That is why I must love my neighbour as myself, because in an important sense my neighbour is myself. And my neighbour, as Jesus showed us in the parable of the Good Samaritan, is anybody in need.

Because of the communion of saints, the mystery of the Body of Christ, because we are all very closely inter-related, therefore none of us can enter into the presence of God simply for himself alone. However and whenever we pray and whatever the form of our prayers, our communion with God always flows out from us to mankind. But since mankind as a whole is far too large a concept for our limited imagination, we can't pray with much meaning for all men everywhere. We have to particularize, praying for parti-cular people or peoples, those we love or those in need, individuals whose plight has been brought home to us or collectivities like the peoples of Russia or Southern Africa.

We lift up our hearts to the Lord so that we may become aware of his presence with us and then in God's presence we think of the person we are praying for. Some-times we shall do no more than present him to the Lord, cover him, if you like, with God's presence in a general sort of way. And sometimes we shall feel led to mention some overriding need he has at the moment, he is ill, or depressed or is finding his job difficult or his wife has recently died. We shall just think of his need and not tell God what to do about it. Sometimes he won't be in any particular need, and we may find ourselves just talking to God about him, especially the people we love and pray for always. We talk about his family and children, his work, his strength and weaknesses, his happiness and worries, presenting him to the Lord sometimes in fairly quick detail. And don't let us forget St Paul's word "by prayer and supplication with thanksgiving", teaching us to give thanks for all men. Part of intercession is giving thanks for people, and sometimes our intercession for a person will take the form of giving thanks for him and nothing more. "Thank you God for creating such a wonderful person as Betty or John."

In intercession we pray for the sake of others, not for ourselves. But our intercession inevitably rebounds on us. It rebounds in two chief ways which are mysteriously intertwined – in pain and in joy.

When we present somebody's need or pain to God we must be prepared in some way or other, in some degree or other, to share the pain. I don't mean that we should try to make ourselves artificially miserable, because that would be sheer self-indulgence – few things are so enjoyable as being miserable. Nor do I mean that there will be any literal identity between my pain and the pain of the person I am praying for. There can't be, since our temperaments and circumstances are different. He has got cancer and I haven't. But in the lives of us all there will come uninvited from time to time things which are difficult, disturbing, painful, even sometimes agonizing. And intercession teaches us that these things are not just for ourselves alone.

We can do more with them than grin hard and bear them, though we may have to do that as well. Though probably in a completely different form they can be seen as our share of the pain afflicting the people we are praying for, so that our own difficulty or misfortune or pain or whatever it is can be recognized as a most important part of our prayer for others. Let us say I am in perplexity or distress, some sort of pain, physical or mental. It means that I have at least some small thing in common (perhaps it won't be so small) with John who has just lost his wife or with the persecuted Christians in Russia. And that something in common, my distress of whatever kind, I can use as my prayer for John or for persecuted Christians or whatever it may be. Put it like this: in some small way I have been allowed to share Christ's cross and so has John or those being persecuted. And my realization of our togetherness on Christ's cross is intercession perhaps at its highest.

Jesus on the cross offered himself to God for mankind. Intercession means sharing in that offering of Jesus on the cross for mankind. But with us, because of our limited imagination, mankind has to be represented by particular people or peoples. We can't pray for people unless we are at least prepared to find ourselves in some way or other with them and with Jesus on the cross. So if and when our life really becomes a mess and we find ourselves one wide wound all of us, then let us open our eyes to see the marvellous and sacred privilege which is being granted to us, the privilege of sharing with Jesus in the cost of healing and restoring mankind. It is easy to be selfish about our sufferings. But if we are, they remain no more than a dead end, when they could be the very centre and mainspring of our prayer for others.

But with the pain there is intertwined joy. Sometimes

the joy in intercession is straightforward, because in our prayers we remember people who are happy and full of zest for life and we realize our oneness with them in the Lord. Something of their happiness and zest bounces back on us. We give thanks for them because what they have is really ours too. But more often the joy of intercession is the joy of Christ raised from the dead because he was crucified. It is in the light of the resurrection that we see the cross on which those we pray for are nailed. In sharing the cross with them we also share the resurrection. It means the joy of knowing that nothing in heaven or on earth, nothing in life or in death, can separate us from the love of God. It is the joy of abundant and indestructible life springing out of death itself, and so out of misfortune and suffering.

Part of our own and most other people's pain is their sense of isolation, their sense of being in the last resort alone. "I, a stranger and afraid in a world I never made." In intercession we begin to realize that we are not alone, that in fact we are in living and active communion with all people living and departed. But since, once again, that is too big a concept for our imagination, we know ourselves to be in living and active communion with the people we love or who have impinged upon us in some way or other.

Prayer is communion with God like that between two friends who know each other intimately. In the Bible people are described as the friends of God. The Lord, we are told, used to speak to Moses face to face as a man speaks to his friend, while the Epistle of St James says of Abraham that he was called the friend of God. And there is no need for us to be reminded of our Lord in St John's gospel calling his disciples his friends. But prayer is not only that. It is also awe and wonder and praise. Such awe, wonder, and praise is something we can be caught up in as we join in communal worship in church. But it may sound a bit unreal to describe awe, wonder, and praise as a church service because, as we all know, a church service can often be dull if not depressing. Let us therefore describe the prayer which is awe and wonder and praise as parallel to what we feel when we are confronted with something of superlative grandeur and beauty – a landscape, the ocean rolling in fullest pride, the magnificence of some blazing thunderstorm, the deep tranquillity of a remote countryside, a work of art which fascinates and compels. Such things indeed not only illustrate the wonder, awe, and praise we feel in God's presence. They are true and valid instances of it. For God's transcendence, what in picture language we describe as his being infinitely above and beyond us, is mediated to us by his immanence, by his being there in his transcendent majesty, in the landscape, the ocean, the thunderstorm, the countryside, the picture by Turner or the symphony by Mozart. That is what we mean when we say that we live in a sacramental universe. The world is charged with the grandeur of God. It will flame out.

But not only in what we call majestic and beautiful things. (Prayer in those circumstances is often easy enough.) But at the very heart of Christian prayer and adoration there is the glory of God revealed in the foul darkness of Calvary. And so prayer is also the vision of God in all that is perverted, ugly, cruel, sick, horrible, death-dealing. Prayer is fully facing the loathsome reality of all these evil things and seeing within them the greater reality, the ultimate reality, of God's glory; the transforming, converting, lifegiving power of his love, even in the corpse of a murdered man. Prayer is seeing Calvary, wherever it may be or whatever form it may take, in the light of Easter and its triumphant joy.

Some years ago I was travelling in a third-class carriage from Paris to Chartres and with me in the compartment were a peasant and his daughter of round about twenty. The girl suddenly had a frightful epileptic fit, screaming and convulsing and frothing at the mouth. I was aware only of the horror of it. It was the girl's father who opened my eyes by the tenderness and love and support he gave to his daughter. He was totally concerned for her, compassionate in a completely practical way, without the slightest hint of being a ministering angel or of any other sort of condescension. That was the form his prayer took in those circumstances, and it revealed evil swallowed up by goodness. I realized that I had seen something which not even all the stained glass at Chartres could show me. Our railway compartment had become the house of God and the gate of heaven.

Anybody would have seen that. It was easy. What is difficult is to see the gate of heaven when there appears to be nothing but sickness and evil, without any visible good swallowing it up. Yet that is precisely what prayer often is, seeing him who is invisible, the Saviour, and worshipping him in his glory when the glory is revealed in his sacred head sore wounded, defiled and put to scorn. And the wounds won't all belong to other people. Many of them will be our own wounds, the subtle psychic wounds which lurk in our own depths and which we are often too frightened to look at or even to admit to ourselves, those elements of us which are unlovely because in some way or other in our early days we were unloved and our intrinsic tenderness was violated. Prayer is the recognition of those wounds as the gate of heaven, the places where above all God is incarnate now in us. So that seeing God's healing presence with us in our wounds we bow down before him in wonder and praise and sing in our hearts of his love to the loveless shown that they might lovely be.

There is a superb image of what I am trying to say in Dostoyevsky's *Crime and Punishment*. Marmeladov, a wastrel who has allowed his daughter Sonia to become a prostitute in order to provide the wherewithal to feed his family, is drunk as usual in a tavern and imagines to the publican all the drunkards being summoned before the judgement seat. Marmeladov says: "And we shall all come forth without shame and shall stand before him, and he will say to us: 'You are swine, made in the image of the beast and bearing his mark. But come to me, you also.' And the wise men will say: 'Lord, why does thou receive these men?' And he will say: 'This is why I receive them, oh wise men, because not one of them believed himself to be worthy of this'. And he will hold out his hands to us and we shall fall down before him and we shall weep and we shall understand all things." We shall understand all things. In prayer we enter into the realm of reality and see things as they really are, from God's point of view.

Real prayer leads to action, leads to us doing what we can for people. But it also saves us from fantasies of omnipotence, of imagining that we can do for people what we manifestly can't do, and from the anxiety and guilt-feelings such fantasies evoke. And praying for people also makes us sensitive to their deepest needs which are generally not their most obvious ones. By means of our prayer God succours people in the very centre and core of their being, and that is what they need most.

See also 'God in all and through all', pages 57–61.

New values

The only absolute standard – the meaning of
goodness – agents of resurrection – self-giving and
sexual ethics – more than one pattern of sexual
chastity – good parents as exemplars of emotional
chastity – intellectual chastity – the riches of
poverty – fulfilment through obedience – the
impossibility of always behaving ideally in an
imperfect world.

The only absolute standard I find in the New Testament is Agape. And Agape converts people by accepting them as they are, as Jesus accepted Zaccheus and the thief on the cross. It was the pharisees who objectively stated their standards of right and wrong with a certainty which led them in the end to crucify the Righteous One. For to equate our own understanding of truth (including moral truth) with the Truth which is God alone is one of the most dangerous forms of idolatry.

Jesus, it is universally admitted, taught no general moral principles. He once used a contemporary summary of the Law – Love God and neighbour – when asked what was the most important commandment. But otherwise his ethical teaching consisted of so many concrete examples of how the power of resurrection could be brought to bear on people in whatever straitjacket they happened to be. Did a man's deadness impel him to take his revenge on life by striking you on the cheek? Then turn to him the other cheek as well. Did his deadness lead him to assert alleged rights over your shirt and begin suing you for it? Then give him your coat as well. Did a petty tyrant seek satisfaction by forcing you to go one mile? Then go with him two. Did a ne'er-do-well take you for a fool who could be tricked into giving or lending him money? Then give it to him without more ado. If a man curses you, return him benevolence. If he treats you badly, treat him well.

To be raised from the dead is to be no longer the prisoner of one's environment. It is to be free from the chains of one's conditioning, past or present. It is to realize that it is not necessary to play the game which is being played on us, so that we can play our own game not the one imposed. That is the secret so far unlearnt by those who despitefully use us. They react to life as life has treated them. They are bloody because life is bloody. Our refusal to play their game may be for them the beginning of a discovery – that like us they are free to be their own master and to live their own life, and not to be merely the sport and toy of circumstance, with everything they do automatically dictated by what is done to them. That such behaviour is to share with God in his work of creation, to participate actively in the creative processes all around us, is explicitly stated by Jesus: "Love your enemies and pray for those who persecute you, that you may be the sons of your Father who is in heaven; for he makes his sun to rise on the evil and on the good, and sends his rain on the just and the unjust."

It is the man raised up from his own dead past who is able by what he is to raise up others from theirs. That is what goodness means. That is the first and final principle of ethics. Ethical behaviour is not submitting to a scale of values. It is magnificently and gloriously to *be*, and in being to create. Ethical behaviour is thus the result of miracle . . . and it is a miracle which at sundry times and in divers manners happens to almost everybody.

What does a person exist to do? A person exists to be the agent of creative goodness. When we thus create goodness we are both ourselves raised from the dead and also the agents to others of resurrection. For genuine goodness always brings life. In the last resort ethics can only be resurrection.

Christians have always everywhere agreed that God is love, and that therefore generous self-giving love is the ultimate moral value. Where the reassessment is necessary is in our understanding of how and when we give ourselves and how and when we refuse to do so. This makes it impossible to describe certain actions as wicked and others as good. For only I myself can discover in what actions I am giving myself and in what actions I am refusing to give. Our Lord, for instance, gave himself by not escaping from martyrdom. St Cyprian, we may believe, would have been withholding himself had he not escaped from the Decian persecution. Or we could consider, as an extreme instance, the act of killing other people. Given certain circumstances, such as war, a man may be convinced that the only effective way in which he can give himself is to steel himself to the task of systematic killing. Another man, in the same circumstances, may be equally convinced that he can give himself effectively by refusing to kill. Or we can imagine circumstances when to steal would be a greater virtue than not to steal. One of the unemployed, before the days of social security, having appealed in vain to all quarters, might have stolen money from a rich man in order to feed his starving family. But suppose he had played a trick upon himself. He wanted to steal the money, but was too frightened to take the risk. He preferred starving his family to the disagreeable consequences which would follow the possible discovery of his theft. His motives show him to be withholding himself. But he can persuade himself that this is not the case. He can pose to himself as a moral man who keeps the commandments. The truth, however, is that what he thinks of as his morality is a disguise for cowardice.

A great deal of what Christians often call virtue, on closer inspection turns out to be cowardice of this kind – a refusal to give myself away because I am too frightened to do it. This is most obviously true in the sphere of sexual ethics, because here more than anywhere there seems to be an enormous amount of double-think. If I am to give myself away to another person, I cannot, in any circumstances, exploit her or him. To exploit is to withhold. It is totally incompatible with giving. But this is not at all the same thing as saying that in certain specifiable circumstances I must always be exploiting and never giving. Yet this is what the Church says about sexual intercourse outside marriage. Such intercourse may be often, perhaps almost always, an exploitation, unilateral or mutual. But there are cases where it need not be and isn't. Incidents in two recent films may be taken as examples. The first is a Greek film, *Never on Sunday*, about a prostitute in the Piraeus. She is picked up by a young sailor. In her room, he becomes afraid, nervous, and on edge. This is not because he thinks he is embarking on something wicked, but because he distrusts his capacity for physical union. He is a prey to destructive doubts about himself, not to moral scruples. The prostitute gives herself to him in such a way that he acquires confidence and self-respect. He goes away a deeper fuller person than he came in. What is seen is an act of charity which proclaims the glory of God. The man is now equipped as he was not before. Can Christians possibly say the devils were cast out of him by Beelzebub the Prince of the devils?

The second film is English – *The Mark*. It tells of the rehabilitation into normality of a man strongly attracted to small girls. His abnormality, which can do nothing but untold harm to everybody, is due to his fear of commitment to an adult woman. However, in time, a woman of his own age inspires him with enough confidence for them to go away for a weekend together. They have separate rooms at the hotel. But it is clear that until he sleeps with her he will not have established enough confidence in himself to

deliver him from his utterly destructive abnormality which
tends to exploitation to the nth degree. Will he be able to
summon up the necessary courage or not? When he does,
and they sleep together, he has been made whole. And
where there is healing, there is Christ, whatever the Church
may say about fornication. And the appropriate response
is – Glory to God in the Highest. Yet each of the men in
these two films might have disguised his fear by the cloak of
apparent morality. Like the pharisees in the gospels and
many good churchmen today, they might have been the
victims of unconscious hypocrisy, keeping the law as an
insulation against the living God, the Creator.

Must not all of us have the courage of Jesus and
address ourselves in his words – "It is written, but I say
unto you"? The risk is admittedly appalling. But Our Lord
warned us continuously that unless we are prepared to risk
everything, we shall never find our lives.

The task of discovering for yourself what chastity means
in sexual matters is no easy option. It is one of life's greatest
challenges, and different people, because they are different,
will make different discoveries. But the aim will be constant
and identical for everybody – the search for integrity and
wholeness as we refuse to evade the question: "Is what I am
doing or propose to do, in the long run life-giving or death-
dealing? And can anything I do be in the long run life-giving
to myself if it is death-dealing to somebody else?" Of
course you can get kicks, a veritable explosion of temporary
excitement and pleasure, by being prepared, if necessary, to
wound another person. But by being prepared to wound
another unnecessarily, you are wounding yourself even
more, for you are making yourself callous, and the callous
man or woman can never be the whole man or woman. For

his or her callousness is a denial of his or her humanity. We are sometimes told that life is for living, which of course is true – so long as we don't silently add a few words to the phrase: "Life is for living, as the wolf said to the lamb."

In working out the meaning of sexual chastity, part of our unavoidable difficulty at the moment is that we have lived through a revolution probably more momentous than any which has formerly occurred to the human race. Within the last half century or so man has acquired both the rational power and the invented means to decide whether he shall or shall not reproduce. An easy form of contraception will soon be a hundred per cent safe. This fact is bound to have some effect, probably a very profound effect, upon our understanding of sexual chastity. When in the second book of the *Summa* St Thomas Aquinas said that fornicating was a mortal sin because "it tends to the hurt of the child to be born of such intercourse" or because "it is contrary to the good of the offspring", his statement is irrefutable. But those conditions no longer obtain, and we have the task of thinking the matter out afresh on new premises.

Many perceptive people, capable of thinking clearly and honestly, have argued as follows. To be fully themselves most people need to establish communion with another person on the deepest possible level. There is a sense in which that communion is given to the couple concerned, but there is also another and vitally important sense in which the communion has to be worked for and earned, just as, to take a parallel, you may be born with the makings of a great pianist, but have none the less to work hard and perseveringly to fulfil your promise. The hard work and perseverance needed to establish communion on the deepest level with another person consists of fidelity, being prepared to take the rough with the smooth, being ready to have your illusions shattered and replaced by reality, and finding the reality of your mutual relationship deeper and more rewarding than the superficial illusions about it with which you started off. All this requires from both the parties concerned a high degree of courage, imagination, perseverance, fidelity, steadfastness and loyalty, as all the best gifts in life always do. It is in these ways that you have to earn and work for the deep communion with another which you need to be fully yourself. But the chief vehicle and expression of that communion is sex. Whatever other forms it takes – and they will be many – your communion with each other must be worked out in sexual terms, and it is therefore in terms of sex that you will need to show that fidelity and steadfastness and loyalty which are the *sin qua non* of deep communion. This points to a permanent and exclusive sexual relationship between one man and one woman as the road to communion and hence to satisfying selfhood for both parties. That, therefore, is the meaning of sexual chastity.

I believe the arguments here to be valid and the conclusions true. At the very least, if we wish to be realistic and sincere, we must weigh up those arguments with the greatest care. Far from being a hard and fast and inhuman rule, they invite us to be human and show us how we can be so. Above all, they make clear the positive and life-enhancing nature of sexual chastity.

On the other hand, I don't think we can confine sexual chastity to one pattern alone, even if it is the pattern for most people. For one thing, is it always the case for every-body that sex as the permanent, self-giving kind of relation-ship I have described is inevitably damaged by other uses of sex? What, for instance, of the sexual liaisons which last for a time, break up, both the parties concerned eventually marrying other people? As a priest I have had the opportunity of weighing a considerable amount of evidence, and what I want now to avoid above everything is humbug. When the liaison breaks up it can cause great suffering and heartbreak to one of the parties concerned, and that possibility should never be forgotten when a man and woman enter a liaison. Nor should the man forget that as an emotional being a woman functions in a different way to a man and according to a different pattern — and vice versa — so that the woman or the man may become more deeply involved than her or his partner. I have seen both women and men permanently injured by what started off as a fairly light-hearted affair whose temporary nature was intellectually understood. But honesty compels me to admit that in my experience this has by no means always been the case. I have seen affairs break up by a consent which was genuinely mutual and with no hearts broken. I have also seen not a few men and women recover from their heartbreak (however shattering it was at the time), fall in love with somebody else, and contract a marriage which was extremely happy and fulfilling. I have also seen sexually inexperienced people rush into marriage without realizing how unprepared for it they were, so that their infantile fantasies were broken up by the hard facts of marriage itself. And that has led to the greatest possible unhappiness and bitterness which, one can't help thinking, might well have been avoided had the parties concerned had more experience of what they were up to, the situation by then being even more complicated by their having children.

There seems in this matter to be no rule which can be applied without exception. Different things appear to happen to different people. Yet what is always needed — and here there is no exception whatsoever — is a sensitive and intelligent concern for the well-being of the other. I have always to ask myself: "Am I exploiting somebody or allowing her (or him) to exploit me?" For to allow yourself to be exploited is to do as much injury to the other as to exploit her or him yourself. True, exploitation doesn't vanish by magic simply because you have had the marriage-service read over you. Yet marriage does provide a frame or context in which the various degrees of exploitation can be recognized, worked through and resolved. Most of the people I know are happily married because they have allowed their marriage to do precisely that for them. It is by growing in realism, growing in their recognition of what is not love or less than love in their relationship, that they have grown in true love for one another.

In the context of our discussion we must remember that quite a number of men and women are by inclination homosexual. Most people are bi-sexual in the sense that their inclinations are 50–50 or 60–40 or 80–20, one way and the other. But I am speaking now of men and women whose inclinations are *predominantly* homosexual. It is easy for a man who is 80 per cent heterosexual to imagine that the man who is 80 per cent homosexual is confronted by a choice similar to his own, and to despise him for not suppressing his homosexual tendencies. But suppressing 20 per cent of your sexuality is, of course, very different from suppressing 80 per cent of it or more. And for a person who is predominantly homosexual to marry somebody of the opposite sex is in most circumstances, to say the least, an extremely unkind, if not brutal thing to do. It is true that both because of its inherent nature, and still more perhaps because of the organization of society, a steady homosexual relationship is very much more difficult to maintain than a steady heterosexual one. But I have seen permanent homosexual unions which are fulfilling to both parties, in which sex has been used as the vehicle and expression of deep personal communion. I have seen it lead in both the people concerned to a wholeness and integrity of character which previously was lacking. When that happens, what are the reasons for doubting that the union is an expression of sexual chastity?

In any case, whoever you are and whatever your sexual inclinations, chastity is an ideal, and it need not be fully achieved in order to be truly present. Like generosity, for instance, chastity is not a matter of all or nothing. It is almost always a matter of degree, though the more chaste you are the nearer to selfhood you will have travelled.

Emotional chastity consists of the attempt to discover our own genuine deep feelings and of being loyal to them even when temporary feelings of an opposite but more superficial kind bang noisily about within us.

Good parents of small children, for instance, always seem to me to have an incredible degree of emotional chastity. I like to think that I myself am fond of small children, and in the abstract I often feel thoroughly sentimental about them. When I visit former pupils and their little children lisp my name I am often very close to tears. But one undiluted hour of their company is enough to change my feelings completely. I find myself giving bad marks to parents who don't realize that their children are a bloody nuisance to visitors, and the only thing which enables me to continue putting on a show of benevolence is the certain knowledge that the children will be safely upstairs in bed before we sit down to dinner. The parents, on the other hand, go on loving and caring for their children however much noise they make or however great a nuisance they are. Parents, I notice, are often tired, irritated, even exasperated by their children's ceaseless antics and tantrums, but they don't capitulate to such feelings. They realize how superficial the irritation or exasperation is compared with the depth of their love. And their love is shown, not in easy tears like mine, but in their willingness to submit themselves on their children's behalf to continuous inconvenience. In this context the parents are emotionally chaste while I am the exact opposite.

The luxury of easy and evanescent emotion is one of the hallmarks of unchastity in the realm of feeling. It was therefore for chastity that Oscar Wilde was pleading when he said that a man would have to have a heart of stone not to laugh at the death of Little Nell. It is where Dickens, like any other novelist, becomes emotionally unchaste that he becomes embarrassing or boring. The death of children seems to have given him particular pleasure. His revelling shows up his feelings here as bogus. He appears to know nothing about the real and devastating pain which bereavement of this kind inevitably brings. Instead we are invited to shed a tear or two and feel good.

What the undiscerning condemn as degenerate and corrupt in contemporary novels, plays and films, is often in fact emotional chastity, the portrayal of real feeling instead of the saccharine concoctions of sentimentality or the undisciplined gushing of romantic rubbish. Often, but by no means always. For there is an artificial bitterness as well as an artificial sweetness. When horror, cruelty, violence and cynicism are revelled in with easy pleasure, and we are not to the slightest degree purged by pity and fear, then there, if anywhere, you have emotional unchastity. Far from really feeling the sharp and savage stab of destructiveness, we are no more than diverted and entertained.

But perhaps, after all, it's not too bad if, as we watch, we are aware all the time that we shall soon be making the Bournvita and going peacefully to bed. For easy, evanescent feeling is at its worst when we fail to recognize its evanescence. That is the commonest kind of emotional unchastity, amusingly portrayed in George Macdonald's description of two silly young women: "They had a feeling, or a feeling had them, till another feeling came and took its place. When a feeling was there, they felt as if it would never go; when it was gone, they felt as if it had never been; when it returned, they felt as if it had never gone."

But emotional unchastity is not confined to evanescent feeling. It can consist also in a permanent feeling, and it is in virtue of the feeling's permanence that the state of affairs I am describing is popularly called a fixation. When I am fixated on something or somebody I have abdicated my personal identity and imagine I am no more than the feeling which has made me its slave. It can be a steely cold feeling as inhuman as ice, as when a man imagines that he is no more than his ruthless lust for power. He kills off everything human in him – his capacity for affection, loyalty, good faith, truth, love, laughter, fun – he kills them all off in order to identify himself totally with his insatiable greed for domination. Or the feeling for which I abdicate my personal identity can be hot and passionate, as when I imagine that there is nothing whatever to me apart from the public cause which I have espoused with an idolatrous devotion. I am not myself because, shall we say, I am *only* my boiling concern for social justice. It is not public spirit which turns people into bores, but the swamping of their identity by the campaign. It is their sin against emotional chastity which makes an evening with them so extremely heavy going.

Religion, unfortunately, is in this context one of the largest and most fertile seedbeds of sin. For, instead of worshipping the true God who gives and establishes my personal identity, it is easy enough for me to worship an idol which robs me of identity and puts its own ugly self in my place. Then, in the name of religion, I want to reduce everybody else to my own nonentity so that my idol's empire may be further extended. Of course I can call the idol what I like and will doubtless give it a most respectable name: Buddha, Marx, Christ, or what you will. It was because Bernard Shaw suspected that, under the stress of war, Nancy Astor was in danger of sinning against emotional chastity that he wrote to her in 1942: "You exaggerate the value of the Christ-like. . . . You yourself have quite as much Christ in you as is good for you." With which we may compare Conrad's cook on board the *Narcissus* who, at the height of a dangerous storm, was "prayerfully divesting himself of the last vestiges of his humanity". The corruption of the best is the worst. When I corrupt what should be my communion with the source of life itself by making it into an agency to rob me of life, then the worst has occurred. The sin against emotional chastity, in its religious disguise, can sometimes look horrifyingly like the sin against the Holy Ghost. "When the light which is in thee be darkness, how great is that darkness."

Intellectual chastity is not something negative, a nagging prohibition. It is our only highway to the facts, to the truth, to things as they really are; and to the sincere and simple expression of what we believe to be true – sincere and simple because we have taken the trouble both to be adequately informed and also carefully to think out the implications of what we have learnt.

Our intellectual chastity may indeed lead us to the conclusion that we can be certain of very little, but that is a more healthy state of mind than being firmly convinced of a whole set of illusory certainties. For we cannot grow into full human selfhood on a diet of illusions. In any case, our intellectual chastity will give us access to reality enough and to spare and will supply us with more than all the nourishment we need, nourishment which, without chastity, would be inaccessible to us because we should fail to recognize it for what it is. Intellectual chastity is the power to discriminate and therefore to see what is what. It is thus the only road to intellectual integrity, and, without intellectual integrity, selfhood runs to seed and we become the victims either of convention or of ideological propaganda, political or what calls itself religious.

Poverty as a positive quality means the recognition that in the most real sense the world is mine, whoever owns it in the narrow technical sense. Poverty is thus the ability to enjoy the world to the full because I am not anxious about losing a bit of it or acquiring a bit of it. Poverty takes pleasure in a thing because it is, and not because it can be possessed. Poverty is thus able to taste the flavour of life to the full.

Suppose, for instance, that you are of a mechanical turn of mind. Any object of engineering skill gives you aesthetic pleasure – you enjoy it for what you see as its beauty. Well, it so happens that your friend George owns a very special car which you recognize at once as a superb piece of craftsmanship. The car gives you pleasure for what it is in itself, it fills you with delighted admiration. Your experience is richer for having looked over it, driven in it, and seen how beautifully it goes. You are glad that such a car exists. In this sense the car is yours, and the fact that it happens to belong to George rather than to you is not so very important. Of course you would like to have one too, but the fact that you don't doesn't spoil your joy in what you admire as a fine piece of work.

That is how poverty makes the world your own and brings you riches. Although all you can afford is a second-hand bone-shaker, you are in fact much richer than Mr Smith down the road who possesses two cars like George's. For Mr Smith bought two, not because he appreciated their quality, but because he wanted to outdo the Joneses next door who have only one. Mr Smith thinks you are poor, and he is right. What he doesn't realize is that in your poverty you are far richer than he is. For the special car is yours in a way that the two cars can never be his.

But perhaps it is with regard to painting and sculpture that poverty comes most naturally to us. I think that is because the price of a great work of art is so astronomical that it is totally out of the question for us to buy and possess it. If we were multi-millionaires our attitude might be more ambiguous. Then let us thank God we aren't, since this means that we can enjoy the picture or sculpture with undivided attention, without plotting how to acquire it or being jealous of those who have. Last year, for instance, there was an exhibition in London of pictures by Lucien Freud whom I believe to be a painter of genius. All the pictures were privately owned, but I doubt whether that was felt as a grievance by the people who went to the exhibition. It was the pictures themselves which completely occupied their attention. They were glad that Freud had been able to paint such pictures. That, for them, was everything, because in the context of the gallery they were walking in the way of poverty.

An important part of poverty, therefore, is the ability

to enjoy things to the full because you can give them your undivided attention, and it is in your giving them such attention that they in their turn give themselves to you. That is how they are yours even though you don't possess them.

But poverty consists of more than the ability to enjoy things unambiguously, however life-enhancing that is. Poverty also consists of the recognition that I have within my own being resources ample enough not simply to cope with life but to meet it creatively, so that it builds me up into my full human selfhood. Poverty is faith in myself as my own bank where I always have at my disposal a balance big enough to live richly and vitally and not to stagnate.

That may sound a strange description of poverty unless I realize that this inner wealth is not a possession which I can hoard and inspect as a miser hoards and counts his money. It is not, therefore, something about which I can be proud or over which I can gloat, for my inner wealth is put at my disposal only as and when I need it. It becomes accessible only as the occasion demands. Poverty is thus always a test and exercise of faith. Because the resources within me are always only latent, I must be content to have nothing until the moment of need arrives. For it is only the need which will actualize what, all unknowingly, I have it in me to be and to do. That is why hypothetical questions about myself are meaningless. What would I be like if in a crisis it really did all depend on me? I can't answer (except bogusly with a false humility or a false pride) because the bank which is myself never sends me a statement of account. I have to learn to live without any known or ascertainable resources at all, simply trusting that as my days are, so shall my strength be. Such a faith is not, of course, in any way a guarantee that I shall always succeed in what I undertake to do. But it does mean believing that whether I succeed or fail, I can win from the experience of success or failure the power to become my own self more effectively and more satisfyingly.

If people are spoilt either by success or failure – as they often are – it is because they haven't learnt that they are poor nor understood the meaning of their poverty. Thus success puffs them up as if by some clever effort their ego had acquired a fortune and failure deflates them as if they had been declared a bankrupt with no reserves of any kind left at all. But poverty understands both success and failure as occasions for our inner and latent resources to be actualized so that they can assimilate either the success or failure as spiritual vitamins which can further our growth into satisfying selfhood. Poverty understands that I am not my success and that I am not my failure, but that both are no more than food which can nourish what I really am – a being who has nothing and yet possesses all things. To the extent that I know that I am thus poor, to that extent I can live without worry and without fretting. "Do not be anxious about tomorrow", said Jesus. It is poverty alone which makes that advice possible to follow.

Fundamentally obedience consists of discovering what you most truly and deeply are or, better, what you have it in you to be, and of being loyal to the insight you have thus received. Such loyalty, as we shall see, may sometimes, perhaps often, involve a degree of submission to some external authority or other. But its root is not submission to anything external, it is being true to yourself.

One of the best examples of obedience in its purest form is the creative artist. He has the immense labour – and often the terrifying ordeal – of discovering what is stirring within him, of catching it, and of expressing it to the utmost limit of his ability. Such obedience to inspiration requires the sternest of discipline. It requires courage, patience, perseverance, faith, the capacity to put up with disappointment and frustration when the thing simply won't come right, the willingness to tear it all up because the vision hasn't come through properly or been adequately expressed, and the no less taxing excitement when the inner stirring is at last captured and satisfactorily stated. All that is what the creative artist has to endure as a matter of obedience to himself. But it is only by such obedience that he can enter into life and take to himself the glorious liberty which belongs to the children of God. Critics sometimes sneer at the idiosyncrasies of great creative artists – at Proust, for instance, for his neurasthenia and cork-lined room – because such critics are too shallow to understand the cost of an artist's obedience to what is in him. But what do their sneers matter compared with what the artist achieves, compared, since we have just mentioned him, with the rivetingly wonderful world Proust created for all time? In obedience to his cross Proust found life – and gave it to mankind.

Ordinary people, like you and me, have to show the same sort of obedience if we are to fulfil our human destiny. We have within us a host of competing claims upon our time and attention, and we have to use both our intuition and our reason to sort them out and arrange them in some kind of order of importance. If, for instance, I have the makings of a scientist or historian and spend all my time at parties or chattering with friends, then my failure to work is a failure in obedience to myself. Or if, to take the opposite situation, I spend all my time working and never see anybody or go anywhere, then I am being equally disobedient to what I am, since by nature man is a social animal and needs company. Or, to take an absurdly simple example, we all know the old song: "It's nice to get up in the morning, But it's nicer to stay in bed." When the alarm clock goes, my immediate impulse may well be to turn it off, pull the bedclothes around me and go to sleep again until lunch time. But if I always do that, I shall cater only for the lazy man inside me and thus be disloyal to that nine-tenths of myself that requires me to get up and be active.

It will be seen that obedience to myself is not at all the same thing as caprice, always giving way to the whim of the moment. On the contrary, it is a yoke and a burden. Yet when we take them upon us we discover that our yoke is easy and our burden is light, for by means of our obedience we are becoming what we are and finding fulfilment, and that is always satisfying. If a man is a mountaineer he may well cheerfully accept the most severe hardships, dangers and privations in order to climb Everest. His is indeed a hard obedience. But it is also an easy one, for he is doing what he is, and that is always the hallmark of true obedience. So it is said of Jesus, the representative man, that for the joy that was set before him he endured the cross. By his obedience to what he was he became fully himself. And there is no other kind of joy.

Part of Christ's cross consisted in the sheer impossibility of doing the ideal thing. Christians have always believed that Jesus was without sin. His actions were never motivated by any selfish desire for gain. But even if you are yourself personally sinless, you cannot help being involved in a society very far from perfect. And your involvement in it will considerably curtail your liberty to do the absolutely right thing. What is right from one point of view seems to be wrong from another. Pay Peter and you deprive Paul. In the end you seem to be left with little more than common sense to decide what you feel to be very profound moral issues. And whatever you decide, it seems wrong somewhere. It's unfair to somebody. It may well injure somebody else. It is far from ideal. Of course, this doesn't mean to say that Christians haven't a duty to do everything they can to inform themselves of the facts and possibilities of any moral question, and to make the best decision possible in the light of what they have learnt. That goes without saying.

What I'm trying to point out now is that, after all this has been done, there often remains a result which is morally unsatisfactory. You may feel, for instance, that it is right for you to give your children as good an education as you had yourself. And for financial reasons, this may mean your having a very small family. On the other hand, this may appear selfish. Perhaps you ought to have a larger family and do them less well. But wouldn't this be wrong?

Christians believe that Jesus took upon himself the sin of the world. I suspect that this has a very profound meaning, known only to the saints. But it also means that Jesus was willing to be involved in the moral unsatisfactoriness of life in society. His teaching shows us how clearly he perceived the absolute ideal of conduct and how completely compelling he found it. (The poetic simplicity of the Sermon on the Mount shows that.) But the history of his mission and death shows us how he was unable to express perfectly in practice the ideal he saw so clearly. He could not do so for reasons beyond his own control. And this was one of the ways in which he carried the world's sin. It was a very real part of his cross — a part he bore with courage and faith. With courage, because he never allowed it to take the edge off his mission. He was not defeated by it, even though a person morally sensitive as he was might well have been paralysed by it into inactivity. Nowhere does he give the impression of a man weighed down by scruples. He accepted his inevitable lot in an imperfect society, and simply pressed on with the work his Father had given him to do. With faith, because he believed that God was equal to the moral contradictions in which the human community is immersed. God had resources enough to overcome them; indeed, perhaps could overcome them precisely by means of their being felt and endured.

This is what Christians believe, in fact, happened when Jesus rose from the dead. We cannot see clearly or fully how. For here and now in history, the moral contradictions continue. It is only beyond history that they are resolved – in the resurrection of the dead. Still, I think we can see this much: the fact that Jesus was often not able to do the absolutely ideal thing was, as I've said, part of his cross. That is to say, it was part of his self-offering. And the self-offering of Jesus was so full that it was large enough to cover all mankind. When he raised Jesus from the dead, God set his seal upon this self-offering and declared that by means of it all the contradictions of human life had been resolved. For the risen Christ was fully man. Nothing of his manhood was left behind when he passed through the grave and gate of death. (That is the significance of the emptiness of the tomb.) But now it was manhood freed from all limitations and contradiction, manhood capable of being absolutely ideal, Jesus's vision of moral perfection completely realized and made actual. When the risen Christ said "All authority is given unto me in heaven and in earth", he was speaking of the love illustrated in the Sermon on the Mount now unreservedly his, at his disposal for ever without check or hindrance of any kind. And by this love, we believe, the world is being redeemed.

This is not something for us merely to contemplate. We are invited to share in it, to make our individual contributions to Christ's redeeming work. And one of the ways in which we can thus share in Christ's work is by facing our inability to do the ideal thing with Christ's own courage and faith. To accept it as inevitable: yet not with stoic resignation, but as an opportunity to share Christ's cross, to make his self-offering our own. We shall not feel that we're doing anything magnificent. Probably we shall feel merely that life always appears to be something rather chaotic, or worse. But we shall be able to recognize this situation as an important part of our calling as Christians, which is, to follow the example of our Saviour Christ, and to be made like unto him.

Belonging

In relationship with Christ and all mankind –
creativity not conformity in social ethics – Marx,
public action and the power of hidden dedication – all
that we are offered to God for others – the cost of
true identification with another person – when
listening becomes sharing – united with everything
that is.

The Christ who has given his life to me has given it also to the whole of mankind. He is inseparable from the people in whom he lives, and I cannot have him without having them as well.

In social as in individual matters, ethical behaviour or goodness is not conformity to an existing value or the attempt to articulate an existing value. Ethical behaviour or goodness is resurrection. It is bringing creative insight to bear upon a social situation so that whatever in that situation is deadening to human development may be changed into something life-giving. Goodness is the fruit of imagination, the product of life coming to consciousness, and this can happen only in the now and with regard to contemporary situations. What is morally right for a society is not a static unchangeable standard, but something which, because it is alive, grows and changes as fresh social situations call forth fresh creative valuations. Ethical insight as resurrection is like leaven working in dough. It ferments in society, giving it life by continually bringing about the conditions in which people may have the maximum opportunity to find and be themselves – people, that is, as they are now today.

The creative insight is generally called forth as a protest against a state of affairs which has come to be seen as death-dealing. It is generally by means of the protest against what is destructive and wrong that people come to see what is creative and right. "In the long run, situations which are unworthy of man give rise to explicit protest, not in the name of a concept of what would here and now at the time have been worthy of man – a concept already positively defined – but in the name of human values still being sought, and which are revealed in a negative manner, i.e. in those destructive situations which evoke by contrast the values concerned.''*

Where in Britain at the moment we desperately need both the protest and the new moral valuations it calls forth is in the whole business of industrial relations which have become death-dealing to all concerned, not only economically but morally and spiritually. The utter uselessness here of merely applying a moral norm has been proved beyond contradiction. It is useless from any preconceived valuations to say: ''This is right. This is wrong.'' For both management and workers have real grievances and can bring strong arguments to support the justice of their claims. The truth is we have not yet discovered what right and wrong mean in the context of industrial relations and we are waiting for a prophet to be raised up to show us.

This situation in our own day underlines forcibly how ethical insight and behaviour must be a matter of creativity and resurrection and cannot be a matter of conformity. ''There is no right way to organize things in this world – no way which might last for ever and be definitive. Instead, in relation to the whole, everything 'right' is merely a road which must be travelled to reveal what the word 'right' could not mean at the outset.''§ If anybody doubts this, let him remember that St Paul wrote to the Corinthians: ''Were you a slave when called? Never mind'', though they were to accept freedom if it was offered (7:21); and that he sent back a runaway slave to his master (Philemon) even if he exhorted the master to treat him as ''more than a slave'', though he did not ask for his emancipation in the legal sense. And we must not forget that it was on board a slaver that John Newton wrote ''How sweet the name of Jesus sounds''. People who inveigh against what they describe as situational ethics seldom realize the backlash of their own

* E. Schillebeeckx, O.P., *God the Future of Man* (Sheed and Ward, 1969), p. 191.
§ Karl Jaspers, *Nietzsche and Christianity* (Henry Regnery Company, 1961), p. 59.

criticisms. For if ethics were not situational in the sense at least which we have described, we might now be claiming the divine sanction of Christianity for the most barbarous and inhuman régimes imaginable.

Christians who quite rightly follow Marx in his demand for practical results in the management of public affairs are sometimes, in their enthusiasm, led beyond this to the assumption that the only action is observable public action. But that is a denial of the invisible God, or at least it is the absurdity of supposing that he can work only within the confines of the social machinery with which we provide him. It is one thing to be willing to learn from Marx; it is another to make God himself into a Marxist. In the 1970s God still moves in a mysterious way his wonders to perform just as much as he did at Olney in the 1770s. For God himself does not change even if our spiritual sensibilities do.

An incurable invalid who has accepted the pain of his constriction as his share in Christ's cross may do more to establish justice in the world than a host of bustling reformers. By accepting his pain generously and dedicating it freely to God as a continuous prayer for others, the sufferer can be the agent through whom God's creative and transforming love is shed abroad in the world. For God accepts and uses his dedication (however little he may often feel dedicated) to empower others to do great things. The people who in public life help to establish righteousness on the earth are debtors to those who support them by the hidden dedication of their lives. What is here being described is what St Paul called the mystery of Christ's Body, which with him continually dies and, with him, is also continually raised from the dead. That is why St Paul understood that "the weapons of our warfare are not worldly but have divine power to destroy strongholds''. By voluntarily accepting the cruel necessity of his affliction as his share in Christ's passion, the sufferer brings to bear upon the world the power of Christ's resurrection which is his power of making all things new. We need to be reminded of this if we are not, in Rupert Brooke's phrase, to be blinded by our eyes. God still works to change his world for the better by means of the things which are not seen.

By underlining the importance of public action to improve the economic structure of society so that a greater degree of justice might prevail, Marx has expanded our spiritual sensibilities, or at least has reminded Christians of what many of them had forgotten. We can gratefully allow him to do that without at the same time allowing him fatally to contract our spiritual sensibilities in another direction.

In so far as we live for others – I am aware of how little I myself do – but in so far as we live for others, we do so not only by our actions and attitudes . . . but also by (what is inseparable from them) our interior state, what we are and what we experience most deeply inside us. The happiness and misery which come to us, the exulting and the agony, we experience as individuals alone. But they are not for us alone. They are for mankind. When we thank God in our joy or cry to him in our pain, we articulate the prayers of the world – prayers which, for this reason or that, perhaps cannot be articulated in some hearts. So we find ourselves offering our joy or our pain to God to be used to help others.

There have been periods in my life – and it must also be true of all of us here – periods of black despair when the only thing that we could do with our distress was to ask God, however half-heartedly and fitfully, to use it to bring light and peace to others. After all, Christ has called us, invited us, to share his cross. And this doesn't mean merely putting up with it. It means offering it for the salvation of souls. These are extreme moments. But we can do much the same when we are on a more even keel. Talking to people in a pub or at supper we find their most hidden desires for goodness and love revealed beneath the surface of what they say. It may simply be a chance remark or an immediately forgotten exclamation. But they show what the person is feeling after, and in our own hearts, as we continue the conversation, we can seize upon this desire of theirs (hidden to a large extent even from themselves) and articulate it in a silent movement of our heart to God; for it is Christ in them, the hope of glory. It is a revelation of God at work redeeming. It owes nothing to our words or deeds, so the prayer is really an act of worship for God's own goodness and love thus manifested in those we are talking with. It is another way in which we are allowed to participate in the redemptive process.

This identification of myself with another person, in so far as it is real, is a very costly business – in terms of time and energy, obviously. But also in a much more important and difficult way. Let us put it thus. In spite of our Lord's warning that it is easier for a camel to go through the eye of a needle than for a rich man to enter the kingdom of God, we all of us spend a great deal of our time accumulating riches like crazy. I don't mean money or material possessions. The riches we try to accumulate are those of character and personality. We build up an image of ourselves and one of our main concerns is to keep the fabric in good repair, so that we can confidently say to our own private ear, "I am this sort of person. I am not that sort of person." Yet the

structure we thus fabricate is, in spite of our apparent confidence, always in a precarious state. Underneath the confidence is the fear of it tumbling down like a house of cards.
And this fear inhibits us from feeling any real identity with
the man who needs our compassion. For to admit that we
are in important respects identical with him seems like
removing the bottom card from the card-house or giving it a
puff from a pair of bellows. So we treat the other person as
a problem or a case or an opportunity to do good instead of
as a person of like passions to ourselves, thus keeping him
at a safe distance from the image of myself it seems so
desperately important to preserve.

Suppose, for instance, that we come across a kleptomaniac. We may be enlightened enough to realize that
simply to condemn him as a criminal does no good to
anybody. Instead we may think of him and behave towards
him as somebody who has a disease called kleptomania, like
a man who has the measles. But this apparently enlightened, clinical approach is in fact an attempt to prevent
ourselves from perceiving how much we have in common
with him. For his stealing is an attempt to compensate
himself for an intolerable sense of having no value, and this
sense of having no value follows from his never having been
properly loved. Now none of us has been fully loved. It is
true of all of us that in this way or that way, to this degree or
that degree, the love we needed to feel our own value has
been withheld. And so the spectre of valuelessness haunts
us all, waiting to spring. And quite a lot of the things I do
are attempts to avert my gaze from this ghost who would
take from me all reasons for living.

True, my own way of compensating myself for the
threatening sense of valuelessness is not that of the kleptomaniac. I do not go around shoplifting. But I see to it none

the less that I accumulate quite a lot of riches: I'm a good sort, I have friends who like me, I get a First in the Tripos, I have a strong will, I went to an expensive school, I have working-class parents, I have a girlfriend who is acknowledged to be exceptionally pretty, I have had a lot of sex, I am a pillar of the college chapel, I am a man of prayer and people realize I live close to God. Now all this sort of riches builds up an impenetrable barrier between myself and the kleptomaniac. For what he needs is somebody who will relinquish these mirages and brave the appalling desert of valuelessness, where he and I both in fact really are. It is in the acknowledgement of this common bond, in the realization that he and I are in the same hell, that true compassion is born and grows. It is not that I am healthy and he is diseased. We both suffer from the same wounds, and that is how we can meet and communicate with each other.

"There, but for the grace of God, go I" sounds pious, but it speaks not of compassion but of superiority. Compassion says, "There, by the grace of God, I have been and I am." It is in this sense surely that we should understand St Paul's words about Jesus: that God "made him to be sin for us, who knew no sin", or St Matthew's words, echoing Isaiah: "himself took our infirmities, and bare our sicknesses". "Christ", said Calvin, "endured in his soul the dreadful torments of a condemned and lost man." The reason why we fail in compassion is because we are too frightened thus to follow Jesus to the cross, going forth unto him bearing his reproach, filling up our share in his afflictions.

Now I know this may sound masochistic, and there is no doubt that what I have said could be twisted to serve the interests of that kind of emotional disorder. But the Christian experience is totally different. Let me put it this way. The Christian gospel speaks a lot about Good Friday and of its inevitability. But for Christian faith Good Friday is seen in the context of Easter. If Christ died, he died in order that he might be raised from the dead. And in page after page of the New Testament we are told that in so far as we share in Christ's sufferings we are made partakers here and now of his resurrection. This is the great and glorious paradox of Christian experience: that it is by dying that we live, that it is by sharing with Jesus the horror of his agony that we live with him reigning indestructibly in peace. Once we are willing to see and feel the desert in which we live, the desert becomes fertile, bringing forth every tree whose fruit shall be for meat, and the leaf thereof for healing. Once we know that we are poor, the kingdom of Heaven is ours. So when our lot is cast with somebody who is finding his cross, his desert, his poverty overwhelming, we are on holy ground. For it is precisely here that God is present to save, to save us as well as them. So our identification with the other person brings to our lives and to theirs the power, the joy, the victory which is already ours and all mankind's in Christ Jesus Our Lord.

That, I believe, is the message which our age is waiting to hear – a realistic recognition of suffering and evil in the universe, not trying apologetically to pretend that things are better than they are, together with the first-hand affirmation of this suffering and evil as the place where the Son of Man is glorified and with him we and all mankind.

Openness to others takes the form of a patient and profound listening to them, a concentrated attention to them that hears what they don't say even more than what they do say. It is perhaps the hardest work in which we ever engage, but it results in our discovery of their lovableness, hidden though it may sometimes be under successive layers of repellent distortion. And the lovableness we thus gradually discover goes deeper (although it is less obvious) than sexual attraction, though it does not exclude the sexual element, which, if present, makes things easier. But the lovableness is ultimately the God who is in them as he is in us, the God who does not override our personal identities but creates and confirms them. So we don't find the other person lovable or attractive for God's sake (treating God as a third party) but because God in the other person has made him attractive in himself. And because God is the deep centre of both us and the other we find that we belong to each other in the most intimate way. We find that we are more than blood-brothers, most intimately interconnected in the deep places of our being.

Listening may begin as a one-way operation, but it can never be that for long. In the silence of our listening we are communicating implicitly with the other person in a language other than words, and thus revealing to him what we are. And the time will come when our self-revelation will become verbally explicit. Our relationship will cease to be apparently one way, as if we were the Good Samaritan and the other the wounded victim, because we shall realize that in order to be healed the other needs to see our own ugly wounds, to encounter us in our sickness as well as in our health just as we are beginning to encounter him in his health as well as in his sickness. We shall discover that both the sickness and the health are things we have in common, so that both can become a bond between us. And as in this way we share what we are with each other we shall discover that it is in each other that we live.

This can happen with regard to anybody to whom we are prepared to listen and to go on listening. And it thus becomes apparent that each of us belongs to all and all to each. It becomes apparent that we are not isolated self-enclosed units, but that the blood of all people throbs in our own veins as does ours in theirs. And the more a person realizes this fact of his co-inherence in others, the more he becomes his own true self. This, of course, is what St Paul was describing when he spoke of the Body of Christ, for Christ in God's eternal purpose is co-extensive with mankind (and indeed with the entire created universe) – "If one member suffers, all suffer together; if one member is honoured, all rejoice together." It is this oneness with each other that Eastern Orthodox thought expresses when it says that man has one single nature in many human persons. "Experience", says Thomas Merton, "is not mine. It is uninterrupted exchange. It is dance."* And it is in being caught up in this dance of humanity, which is also the dance of the whole created universe, that a person discovers who he truly is.

There is, you see, in the most literal sense no such thing as a lonely soul, only a soul which is blind to the indissoluble ties which unite it with everything that is. Sometimes we're aware of how we thus belong. Confronted, shall we say, with some great scene of natural beauty we're moved to what is in fact the form of contemplation. The mountains or the meadows that we see aren't felt as something alien to us which shuts us out. We feel deeply if inarticulately that we belong, that what we see is an element of our own identity. It's not for nothing that the Bible tells us that the Lord God formed man out of the dust of the ground. This same sense of belonging is true of our work when it goes well. To the scientist or scholar his laboratory or library is not an alien land. He feels truly part of his work, and he's

*Thomas Merton, *Asian Journal* (Sheldon Press, 1974), p. 68.

happy because he knows that he belongs to what he does. Christians would describe these experiences as the presence of Christ who, in St Paul's words, fills all things.

But of course it's with other people that most of us are chiefly concerned and it's communion with other people that most of us want more than anything else. And this desire for communion includes as an inevitable part of it a very deep-seated wish to be of service to others, to help them, to be of use. It's true that this can be used to minister to our own egotism when we want to pose to ourselves and others as saviour figures. I believe in the reality of what some psychiatrists describe as a Christ complex. But the perversion of something good doesn't destroy the reality of its goodness. Helping people often obviously calls for action. But however essential it may often be to take action on behalf of others, it's not, I firmly believe, by action that we help them most. For the outward contact we have with people is no more than the external visible sign of an inward unseen communion.

We can help people most by living for them as Jesus did, offering ourselves to God on their behalf in all we are and do. So the night before he died Jesus prayed for his friends and said, "For their sake I now dedicate myself that they too may be dedicated in truth." If in the silence of our own prayer we sincerely give ourselves to God on behalf of other people, then we can leave specific actions to look after themselves. We'll do them all right and what's more we shall prevent ourselves doing more harm than good. In any case, people in the deepest need are in the last resort unapproachable on the level of external contact. But just as Jesus accepted his approaching death, we can accept some handicap or disappointment or frustration or duty that has come our way, and pray to God of his loving kindness to use it to bring help to the afflicted or joy to those we love, or peace on earth. The truth of our interconnection has been well described by the French writer Léon Bloy in his own poetic idiom: ''An impulse of real pity sings the praises of God from the time of Adam to the end of the world. It cures the sick, consoles those in despair, calms the raging of the sea, ransoms those in prison, recovers the lost and protects mankind.'

But as members one of another in Christ we're not only donors. We're much more recipients. When, after a period of darkness, light floods into our hearts, when some load is shed, when we have been enabled to do the right thing, when if you like we recover a lost sense of belonging, isn't all that because we do in fact belong, with the result that spiritual and moral victories achieved by others have come to our rescue and stood us on our feet? ''No one lives and no one dies for himself alone'', says St Paul. This deep interpenetration of all souls with each other is in the Christian vocabulary called the communion of saints. That phrase doesn't refer to a huddle of pious people. It means that we're all one in Christ, that in Christ we belong intimately to each other, that there is a continuous and mutual traffic between us all, that as an individual person I belong to everybody who has ever lived and that they belong to me.

To our ordinary way of thinking that may sound fantastic. But our mind is a limited instrument and it's only common sense that we can't empty the ocean into a bucket.

In so far as in our inmost being we grasp the truth that in Christ all things are ours, whether this person or that person or the other person or the world or life or death or things present or things to come, in so far as we grasp that all things are ours, we shall be happy with a happiness of which literally nothing can rob us.

See also 'Prayer', pages 155–59.

Creative uncertainties

The human vocation – the distresses of choice – the
acceptance of mixed motives – the price of
creativity – love and hate – fighting the God on whom
we depend – aggression as an expression of love – of
images and Reality – atheists for the love of God? –
living with contradictions – freedom in the acceptance
of necessity.

In the New Testament the cross is more than once described as a conflict, as a creative conflict which leads to resurrection. The vocation of being human is a vocation to enter into that creative conflict and make it our own. It is true that to each individual person the call to conflict will come in a particular way. But behind that particular call is the general one to recognize and accept and welcome the life-giving cross in each and every department of our lives.

In our actions, our circumstances and disposition severely limit the number of possibilities open to us, and far from choosing to do the ideal thing we shall most often find ourselves compelled to choose between courses of action all only moderately good, or between the least of several evils. That, after all, is what Jesus had to do. He had to choose between disappearing from the scene or aggressively challenging the ecclesiastical authorities in a way which was certain to evoke their counter-aggression. And wasn't that choosing the lesser of two evils?

But our finitude not only limits the possibilities open to us. It demands of us that we do one thing rather than another. It confronts us with an either/or. That means that during our life there will be many doors accessible to us which we never opened, many roads we could have walked down but didn't. We can't, for instance, be both men of learning and also pastors available to all in need twenty-four hours a day. We can't give to our family the time they have the right to expect from us *and* live for nothing but our work. We can't both be married and be monks. And so on and so on.

This necessity to choose between an either/or seems a matter of obvious common sense. But in practice it often gets loaded with a considerable degree of irrational guilt-feelings. The doors we never opened and the roads we never walked down seem to rise up and accuse us. "Why", they complain to us, "did you miss the opportunity of opening me? Why did you miss the opportunity of walking down me?" We hear the voice of a person in distress saying to us, "You were so busy studying that you didn't even know I existed." Or we hear the voice of somebody in real intellectual difficulty saying to us, "You were so concerned to preserve your self-image as a pastor that you neglected learning and thus you were utterly useless so far as I and people like me were concerned." If to our irrational guilt-feelings about what we chose not to do we add the common human fallacy that other fields are always greener (because we know from experience the snags involved in what we chose to do and have no experience of the snags involved in what we didn't choose to do), taking all this into account we can begin to see the necessary cross involved in action. Even within the small circle of our limited possibilities we have to choose to do X, and choosing to do X means choosing not to do Y. And the result is both the pain of feeling guilty and the suspicion that we may well have thrown away our chances and missed the bus.

Many people try to escape from this cross by repressing the pain it brings. The result is that they become pig-headed, obstinate, and insensitive in the bogus assurance that they have no doubts about what they do. The courageous man, on the other hand, is willing to bear his cross. He makes decisions and acts decisively once he has made up his mind and he remains firm and consistent in his purpose. But, at the same time, he is open to new points of view and is able to see new facets of a situation because he is willing to bear the burden of his guilt-feelings and his uncertainties. He does not try to run away from them and cover them up, however decisive and consistent his actions may be. It is the combination of decisiveness with the acceptance of himself as fallible, prone to guilt-feelings and in what he decides to do certainly doing harm as well as good – it is this combination which in the realm of action marks the man of the cross.

There is too about him something of the *Pecca Fortiter*. For behind the choices he makes and the actions which follow there lie his motives. I suspect that motives for doing anything are invariably mixed, a combination of generosity and self-concern, and, even more, a combination of a me who is genuinely trying to discover and establish his true identity and a me who is running away and trying to hide from himself. Novelists of perception (Iris Murdoch comes immediately to mind) understand this game which people play with themselves. Its description is the main element in their work, so that we are always at a loss to know who the goodies are and who the baddies. If we are to make decisions and act we have to bear the burden of our mixed motives, acknowledging to ourselves that they are mixed but at the same time going ahead resolutely and acting. When we do this we shall, almost in spite of ourselves, be contributing to the ultimate fulfilment of God's purpose. As Aristotle says in his *Ethics:* ''Truly in each man's heart God lives. And God striving and spreading in him prompts him to strange actions and modes of being unaccountable even to himself. Impulses, fears, contradictions, all unreckonable. Thus under all strife it must be that the whole universe of things is striving, pursuing ever, yet not pursuing what one fancies but the One.'' It is in the light of that understanding that the *Pecca Fortiter* is seen in its true significance and makes us ready to carry the cross of our own mixed motives.

It is when we engage in public, communal, political action that it is particularly important that we should know and admit to ourselves how mixed our motives are. If we believe a state of affairs is wrong, then obviously it is our duty to do what we can to have it put right, and this may well demand of us that we engage in some sort of public crusade or political campaign. Shouldn't we be running away from our vocation if we didn't? Our politics will be a true and authentic attempt to see that right prevails in the world. To eschew politics of this kind may well be the shirking of an obvious duty. At the same time, unless we are to become fanatics, we must recognize that our devotion to the public cause has more sides to it than one. We are the champions of right over wrong: that is one very important side to it. We are seeking self-expression and self-fulfilment by means of the campaign: that is another side to it. The right we are championing is not pure transcendent right but right articulated (as it must be) in terms of a particular campaign. And there will not be general agreement about the degree in which the campaign successfully articulates the transcendent right. We shall, as always, be serving the absolute by means of the relative. That is still another side to it.

The tension involved in all public political action is the necessity to act positively and boldly, to go straight for it, while at the same time realizing that our motives are mixed and that the specific campaign is only a partial and relative, and therefore inadequate, articulation of the everlasting right. If we refuse that tension we shall become either the fanatical devotees of an idol or people of such moral cowardice that we are too paralysed to campaign for the right at all. Above all, whether by temperament we are drawn to public affairs or not we must be clear that the mixed motive, the imperfect articulation of the right in practical terms, while the campaign in its methods if not its objectives will probably be a combination of wisdom and folly – we must be clear that these things do not in the slightest invalidate what people try to do by public action to make the world a better place. Scrupulosity here may merely be a disguise for laziness or simply not caring or more probably fear – the burying of our talent in the ground because we know our master is a hard man.

Did not part of the agony of Jesus in Gethsemane consist in his awareness of the haunting possibility that there may have been some fundamental mistake in the embodiment he had tried to give to the kingdom of God? Tolerance of that possibility is the price which must always be paid for creativity.

The ability to love must involve the ability to hate. If I'm incapable of hatred I'm incapable of love. And because hatred is so unpleasant and disturbing an experience, people try to block off these vital areas of feeling in the name of common sense or even of goodness, as though to be indifferent to somebody were a morally better state than hating them. I remember a character in one of Graham Greene's novels saying: "I would rather have blood on my hands than water – like Pilate." The fact is we can love God and our neighbour only at the expense of also being able to hate both of them. That is what Camus meant when he said that every blasphemy is a participation in holiness. Unless we are ready to entertain this conflict between love and hatred we shall never grow in the love of God or man.

We are entirely dependent upon God, yet at the same time there is a sense in which we must learn to be independent of him. If we are to be truly alive, we must be ready in our relationship with God to accept the conflict between dependence and autonomy. Whatever Bonhoeffer intended, I think that it is in this sense that we must understand man's coming of age. It is not that in the twentieth century mankind has come of age in any evolutionary sense, but that it is God's will that a man should be fully himself; and that if a man is to be fully himself his relationship to God cannot find expression only or exclusively in terms of dependence. If I may . . . borrow from the rabbis, they interpreted Jacob's wrestling with the angel at Peniel as his wrestling with God for a good covenant, for good terms. And because Jacob was not just passively dependent but took the appalling risk of wrestling with God for good terms, he got them. He was blessed "for as a prince hast thou power with God and with man and hast prevailed".

This insight was not unique to Jewish antiquity. You find it also in Greece. Much of Greek drama is concerned with that knife-edge between dependence on the powers that be and the necessity to assert one's own autonomy. Fall either side and you are destroyed. *Hubris* certainly is punished. But you can also fall a victim to mania.

In a nutshell the inner conflict we are concerned with is this: in order to be people and not ciphers we must needs fight that on which we rely.

What does this mean in practice?

Karl Barth once said very characteristically that to call God "Father" is not to speak of God anthropomorphically but to speak of man theomorphically. That is the sort of profound but crude statement allowed to prophets and poets, and Barth was both. The point is put, I think, far less strikingly but with greater finesse by means of the concept of analogy. . . .

. . . since God is the ground of our being, the fount
from which we continually flow, since God is our origin, a
great deal of our basic feelings towards him will be chan-
nelled or conveyed to us by means of the kind of feelings
which a son has for his earthly father. That is to say, the
characteristic ambiguities, conflicts and crises which are
part and parcel of a son's healthy and maturing relationship
with his earthly father will inevitably find their counterpart
in a man's relationship with God. As well as love and
obedience, there will be resentment, rebellion and self-
assertion – the bid, in short, for independence. Conflict of
this kind is absolutely necessary if our relationship with
God is to grow into maturity. And unless this absolute
necessity is recognized, we shall misunderstand what is
happening to us and be weighed down by an appalling load
of guilt; or we shall repress the conflict so that it can find
only a sneaking and perverted expression below the level of
consciousness while we apparently remain God's good little
boys, futile and ineffective half-people.

You may answer that I am speaking only of the
temporary crisis of adolescence. But even on the human
level I wonder how temporary the crisis in fact is? It is true
that Dad probably soon ceases to be a threatening figure to
be resisted, but the father-archetype is by no means
confined to Dad. Think of what some of you feel about the
boss, or, if you are a clergyman, what you feel about
bishops. Think of the pleasure with which, in democracies,
people vote against their rulers. Think of the anger
generated by establishments of every kind. Even on the
purely human level the crisis of adolescence seems to be
active during most of our lives. On the deeper level, a man
would have to be extremely conceited and blind to imagine
he had outgrown his spiritual adolescence, that he was

established enough as a person, that he was sure enough in his independence, completely to accept without conflict his entire dependence upon God. For that claim to be a full-grown man would be a claim to have reached the measure of the stature of the fullness of Christ, and to make such a claim would be in itself an indication of how bogus it is.

Our spiritual adolescence catches us up in a difficult contradiction. According to the laws of all growth, natural and spiritual, our deepest obedience to God our Heavenly Father will require of us the courage of disobedience. Our ultimate "Yes" to God will require us to take the risk of saying "No". Our filial relationship with God, if it is to grow into a mature filial relationship, will confront us with the necessity of rebellion against him. Hence the truth that it is the greatest sinners who make the greatest saints. And we have it stated in one of the most central expressions of Christian experience – the "Felix Culpa" of Holy Saturday and the "absolutely necessary sin of Adam". If the doctrine of original sin is not a description of something which happened literally in the past, then what it does is to stress the inevitable tension in which we are all involved between an ultimate good and a temporary evil. Either we grow or we atrophy and die. If we are to grow, we must, like Jacob, fight that on which we rely. You can put this doctrinally as Tillich did by saying that the creation and the fall are synonymous. . . . whether we like it or not, in our relationship with God we are bound to feel the contradictions and conflicts of our spiritual adolescence. In our own lives we are bound to feel the tension between the creation and the fall. Our obedience to God requires us to fight him. And when we fail in that most radical and paradoxical kind of obedience people smell death in our churches and stay away.

What is really absurd and really blasphemous (since it defies the order of creation) is to imagine that we can love God without at times feeling highly aggressive towards him. There is often more love in a "Christ Almighty" than there is in a spiritually castrated "Alleluia".

In science, theoretical models are partial and provisional ways of imagining what is not observable. They are symbolic representations of aspects of the world which are not directly accessible to us, limited and inadequate ways of imagining what cannot be observed or otherwise reached. So, for instance, I am told that gases are understood according to the model of their being composed of tiny elastic spheres, though it is admitted that the model bears only a partial resemblance to what it attempts to describe and thus remains hypothetical. But being as good a description as has been so far possible, scientists consider it worthy of at least a tentative commitment.

Christian doctrines are like the theoretical models of science. They are neither literal pictures nor useful fictions. Christian doctrines are not a game of "Let's pretend that so-and-so is the case in order that we may lead better and more loving lives". They are an attempt to describe what is really there by the best models available at any time. But the models can provide only partial and inadequate descriptions, and they may speak meaningfully to one age and not to another. And because they are models of this kind Christian doctrines are by nature only hypothetical, and the commitment we can give them is thus only tentative. Doctrines cannot escape reformulation as society changes, just as scientific models cannot escape reformulation as scientific attitudes change. In their form, therefore, creeds are as tentative as scientific hypotheses. The Reality to which they point and which they attempt to describe does not, of course, change.

The difficulty is to distinguish between the unchanging Reality and the changing formulation, to recognize that the Reality does not depend upon the attempted formulation of it. Facing and negotiating that difficulty is one of the ways in which we are called to die to the flesh in order to live to the spirit. And St Paul's remark that the letter killeth while the spirit giveth life is here highly relevant. If we refuse that death to the flesh and treat Reality and its models as one and the same, we become idolaters. For we are treating the human and relative as though it were divine and absolute, which is the quintessence of idolatry. For all our apparent zeal, for all our posing to ourselves as the loyal champions of Christian truth, we should exemplify the people described in the first chapter of *Romans*: "Those who have become futile in their thinking, their senseless minds being darkened, because they have exchanged the glory of the immortal God for images resembling mortal man." And it makes no difference whether the images are metal or mental. We *must* have images but we must sit lightly to them, and we must never confuse the images with the Reality they most inadequately represent.

What I wonder is whether we can truly love God unless from time to time we disbelieve in his existence. I suspect that to love God with all our heart will sometimes, perhaps often, involve us in being atheists. We must not evade the conflict of our atheism. We must be ready to accept the tension of our discovery at certain times that we think the whole Christian bundle of tricks is a lot of bloody nonsense. The last thing God wants is "yes-men", for a "yes-man" is a far deeper denial of him as creator than a man who can say

"No". There are many interpretations of the words from the cross and I know my critical study of the gospels. But I would suggest that one possible line of interpretation is that it was precisely because Jesus had reached the point where he could say nothing else than, "My God, my God, why hast thou forsaken me?" that he was able afterwards to say "*Consummatum est*". It was by his willingness at that point to become an atheist that he consummated his love for God.

We must be loyal to the totality of our experience and accept the fact that it certainly won't fit together in any satisfying scheme of logical coherence. Of course we must always try to fit together as much of our experience as we can, try to make sense of as much as we can, always striving for some sort of coherence, but at the same time we must be ready for our experience to confront us with irreconcilable contradictions, so that often in the same breath we shall have to say of the same thing, "Yes, it is true" and "No, it isn't true". When, for instance, we are told that there is a special providence in the fall of a sparrow, part of my experience tells me it is true and part of my experience tells me it isn't. That is the cross of faith. And at this point we are all apt, like the first disciples, to forsake Jesus and flee by evading or smothering that part of our experience which tells us it isn't true. But real faith, as Jesus showed us on Calvary, consists in accepting the "No, it isn't true", thus recognizing doubt as itself an essential and important element of faith. And I mean real doubt, existential doubt about our own nature and destiny, doubt about where and what we are and where we are going. When we say of ourselves "Yes, we are" and "No, we aren't" it is often impossible for us to tell which of the two statements is the truer.

We are very much hedged in, the victims very largely of necessity. The iron law of necessity operates throughout most areas of our lives. Perhaps of all the conflicts we experience, that between necessity and freedom is the most creative of all. That is more than hinted at by the arts. Art, we say, consists in limitation. If the artist is to give expression to the freedom of his insight, he must submit himself to the necessities imposed upon him by his medium, be it paint and canvas, or stone, or words, or notes. For the artist the necessity of his medium is the vehicle of his freedom. But then art is a contained affair. It is concerned with what you can do simply with paint or stone, etc. In the wide and varied jumble of our lives in general it is far harder to see necessity as the vehicle of our freedom. Yet such it is. We are hedged in by our circumstances and disposition, and our freedom consists in our relationship to them. We may shake our fist at necessity as our foe, and if we do we shall remain its victims. Or we may welcome necessity as our friend and ally, and if we do that, it will be on our side and create us.

Here inevitably we are caught up in the subsidiary tension of discovering if what we took to be necessity really is. If we can change a situation for the better, then we should change and not accept it. If I have tuberculosis I must change it into health by using the drugs for that purpose now available. In such circumstances mere acceptance of the disease would be psychopathological. But when we have discovered that a necessity is really necessary, that it is unalterable and we can do nothing to avert or change it, then our freedom consists in the acceptance of the inevitable as the medium of our creativity. It is in the very thing which compels us that we find our freedom. Great writers, for instance, have often had to write for money to support themselves and their families, and have thereby discovered the wings they possessed to soar in the freedom of their spirit. For to be free is to be fully ourselves, and it is to this becoming and being fully ourselves that we harness the hard necessities laid upon us. We make the necessity serve our purpose as persons just as the sculptor makes the hardness of the stone serve the purpose of his creative vision:

> *In the deserts of the heart*
> *Let the healing fountain start*
> *In the prison of his days*
> *Teach the free man how to praise.*

This acceptance in our lives of necessity belongs to the highest form of action, and is a parallel to that receptive passivity which we have noted as the most valuable part of prayer. When in our lives we accept necessity which is really necessity we are letting go and letting God take on. From this highest form of human action we gradually discover that, after all, we have willed everything which has happened to us. I don't mean willing in the imperious sense of insisting that such and such is done, but the discovery that we wouldn't have had it otherwise, that there is an identity between the willed and the inevitable. What I desire is what I've got. Or as Dante put it: "In His will is our peace."

4

A New Creation

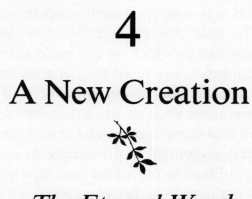

The Eternal Word

The creative Word, the mystery of all things and
fullness of life – openness to the Eternal Word, the
preliminary to present resurrection – God calls and
creates us through our circumstances – disturbances
from the Creator Spirit – living goodness and the
creation of new values – the great artists show us
Reality – continually being created ourselves, we
share in Christ's work of creating mankind.

The Eternal Word is for ever becoming flesh as man's developing self in its entirety is continually being called into being. . . . To hear that creative Word is the authentic spiritual experience by which we are made alive. And life-giving spiritual experience is not one department of life nor one activity among others, but the whole of life in its creative impact upon us as we open ourselves to receive it. . . . It is a spiritual experience which began when we were in our cradle and responded inarticulately to our mother's love. And it continues as our world summons us to respond to it by going out to meet it. The place where we feel most at home, the people we most deeply love, the works of genius which have most fired our imagination, these are instances of the Word being made flesh and dwelling among us, and thus creating us. Each of these instances confronts us with its own mystery. We cannot fully describe or explain any of them. It is in being themselves that they beckon us to communion with them and their final identity is intellectually elusive. If we know them deeply (as we can) we shall hear them say, '*Noli me tangere.*' We shall recognize that they have about them an inviolability which means that a condition of thus knowing them deeply is our acceptance with regard to them of a fundamental unknowing. If we try to overcome this necessity of unknowing by attempting to force our way into their ultimate secret and insisting that they hand over their mystery for dissection, then the place, the people, the work of art, disappear altogether and leave us with no more than an inventory of disjointed fragments.

> *He who binds to himself a joy*
> *Does the wingèd life destroy;*
> *But he who kisses the joy as it flies*
> *Lives in eternity's sun rise.*

To recognize and respect the mystery in all things, to discover thereby that we belong to them as they belong to us, to find our own identity in this experience of intercourse with what is potentially inclusive of all reality, that is to hear the voice of the Eternal Word and to be raised up to fullness of life.

If we cannot raise ourselves from the dead, we can, to some extent at least, unplug our ears to hear the voice of the Eternal Word in things which threaten to turn us upside down and inside out. It may be a television programme. It may be the behaviour of the young. It may be somebody with whom we have fallen in love. It may be some predicament we are in. It may be the strength of our unsatisfied desires. It may be success or failure. It may be a public event which monopolizes the headlines. It may be anything. For in everything we must be open to receive the Eternal Word whose call is both the destruction and resurrection of what we are.

It is above all by the open mind and the open heart, the willingness to abandon even what seem the most sacred of our prejudices, the willingness to think and feel what we are out afresh, it is by that openness, and that alone, that we can work out our salvation. And certainly it will be with fear and trembling. For the unknown threatens before it gives life. The beast roars before we discover that he is Prince Charming himself. This openness requires discipline and courage of a heroic kind, and neither religious devotion nor moral earnestness is any guarantee of its presence. "Watch, therefore, for you know neither the day nor the hour." It is only by being on the alert for change within ourselves that we shall interpret the sign of the times, and so be ready to hear the voice of the Eternal Word.

There is hope here as well as demand. For since the Eternal Word can speak through any and every circumstance, we can never conclude that our own or other people's outward or inner circumstances are altogether too unfavourable for the miracle of resurrection to occur. Charity to ourselves and others requires that we ameliorate those circumstances as much as possible. But when all is said and done it remains true that it is neither promising people nor lucky people nor deserving people nor likely people who are raised from the dead, but precisely dead people. The background of resurrection is always impossibility. And with impossibility staring us in the face, the prelude to resurrection is invariably doubt, confusion, strife, and the cynical smile which is our defence against them. Resurrection is always the defiance of the absurd.

Our physical, emotional, and sexual disabilities, therefore, do not exclude us from the resurrection of the body. They can be the very means whereby the creativity of life takes hold of us. And as it does, we shall find ourselves accepting what we are and no longer wishing we were something else (the content of our waking fantasies). Unless we are literally in the last stages of physical illness we shall discover that what we are can bring its own bodily fulfilment. Only we must not be hypnotized by the stereotypes and their brash assumption that fulfilment can come only within the narrow limits of the images they purvey, or we shall be like a man dying of thirst by a mountain stream because there is no tap for him to turn on. *Eros*, with its roots deep in sexual feeling, can by acceptance be diffused throughout our entire physical structure so that every contact we have with others and the world we live in can be an act of physical love. It requires a miracle. But it is a miracle which has occurred to many men and women, and from which our disabilities in no way exclude us.

If to openness of mind and heart we add a measure of expectancy, then we shall be looking for the resurrection of the body which is the resurrection of the flesh. And if we are thus seeking, must it not mean that we have begun to find?

We often find ourselves thinking — "If only such and such elements in my present circumstances were different, if only I had better health or more time or fewer worries or more congenial companions, then I could serve God better." But that is nonsense. God calls us precisely in and through our circumstances. They form, if we may so put it, a daily annunciation, a daily call from God, to which we can only reply, "Be it unto me according to thy word." But the acceptance of the call is also the discovery of its creative character — "the Holy Ghost shall come upon thee, and the power of the Most High shall overshadow thee. . . . For no word of God shall be void of power".

Whatever God may call us to be and do, by the very fact of the call he will continue in us the mighty work which he wrought when he raised his Son from the dead.

When we are thinking things out to solve a problem or set something in order, it is the Creator Spirit himself at work in us, energizing within the limits and quirks of our human condition, creating the answer by enabling us in our fumbling way to work it out for ourselves.

When, for instance, somebody is writing a book, he may often find it almost impossible to pray in the ordinary sense of being still and receptive in the presence of God, since he cannot help thinking about what he is going to write, whether in what he has already written he has in some place or other expressed himself badly or whether the whole plan of the book needs revising. In those circumstances he must not be misled into fighting against God. For it is God himself, the Creator Spirit, who has set his mind fermenting in this untidy and distracting way.

An old priest who had devoted his life to the people of the East End of London used (as old men often do) to speak his thoughts out loud. To hear him celebrate the Holy Communion made Christianity live for you in laughter and tears. For throughout the service he would proceed thus: "Let us pray for the whole state of Christ's Church militant here in earth. I must remember to see about those turkeys for the old people's Christmas dinner." "Make your humble confession to Almighty God meekly kneeling upon your knees. Perhaps I'd better call again on those damned electricians. They never come when they say they will." He was near enough to God not to be worried by these disturbances from the Creator Spirit.

The essence of human life . . . is to be creative. To say that man is made in the image of God is to say that man shares with his creator in the work of creation. To say that the image is soiled or tarnished is to say that man has lost to some extent his ability to be creative because he has become enslaved to a dead past of some kind so that instead of creating he conforms. The remedy for this state of affairs cannot possibly be the adoption of a new pattern of conformity, however exalted and sublime may be the prefabricated values offered for imitation. Living goodness, in other words, must be the result of renewed creativity, and it will manifest itself not in terms of realizing values which exist already in some changeless ideal realm above and beyond man, but in terms of actually creating values which are new. "The task of ethics is not to draw up a list of traditional moral norms, but to have the daring to make creative valuations."* And values can thus be created only by being lived, not by being argued about or assented to. This creation of new values means that for us to enter eternity and be given eternal life is not to be raised up to the vision of some static state of changeless perfection, but to participate more and more actively in the creative processes we find all around us here and now. To share God's life is to find ourselves creating with him.

To be raised from the dead by the creative call of the Eternal Word is to find that we are ourselves agents of resurrection. And to be ourselves agents of resurrection, raising men from enslavement to their own dead past, is the true meaning of ethical behaviour. Goodness, in other words, is the expression of superabundant life. It is our way of endlessly becoming more and more of what we are, so that other people are enabled to do so also. It is the overflowing of joy – the joy which brings life to everybody it meets.

One of the most curious tricks which religious and Christian people often play upon the God they are supposed to worship is their attempt to keep him out of his own world. They want their rights in him to be exclusive. One example of this can be found in their official list of heroes and great men, those granted the accolade of sainthood. They are all churchmen. You won't find Shakespeare on the list and you won't find Blake or Bach or Beethoven or Turner. When Christians assemble for worship, how often do you hear them thanking God for the vision and inspiration such supreme men of genius have conferred upon

* N. Berdyaev, *The Destiny of Man* (Geoffrey Bles, 1937), p. 20.

mankind? The transcendent glory they reveal to us is simply ignored in our forms of service, ancient or new-fangled.

But God refuses to be victimized by the trick his official devotees try to play on him. Far from allowing himself to be no more than the god of a closed shop, he cuts the shop down to size by pouring the riches of his Reality upon outsiders, revealing himself through the perceptions he gives to the great artists of mankind and which they in turn give to us so that we also in their works perceive the overwhelming grandeur which both confronts us and belongs to us – the chastening power of beauty, the terror which slays and makes alive, the tenderness and steel of love, and in it all, those conflicts which are the agony and ecstasy of man.

It is to honour those who have thus enriched us that this Festival of Music and the Arts* has been organized – to honour them and to enjoy what in their works they seek to share with us. Yet "enjoy" is obviously too weak a word. We enjoy ourselves certainly, but our enjoyment passes into wonder and worship as something of the glory of the Lord is made known to us by what we hear and see – that glory in which awe and intimacy are reconciled and known as one.

Our world stands in the greatest need of what a festival of this kind makes available to us. For living in a scientific and technological age we are in danger of losing our grasp upon the personal. While thanking God for the achievements of science and technology, we must not be blind to the perils of a too exclusive preoccupation with them. It is true that the scientist is original and creative. But, as Teilhard de Chardin has warned us, the scientist's originality it soon swallowed up in the universal nature of the conclusions at which he arrives. His personal creation is soon swamped in the collective creation to which he contributes. Science is the work of a team – a world team, and

* Isle of Man first International Festival of Music and the Arts, 1975.

thus becomes impersonal. The human worker is cancelled out by his work. But in the arts every work of creation is unique and continues to bear the hallmark of its creator. The unrepeatable individuality of a Blake or a Beethoven shines through all their work, reminding us and reassuring us of the supreme importance of the personal. People, they convince us, count infinitely more than things.

That word "infinitely" is not here being used in a loose sense. For the artist shows us how a human person can in his very individuality be the agent of what is eternal and universal. It is in terms of his unique personhood that he reveals to us truth which is always everywhere truth, and beauty which is always everywhere beauty. He catches the Infinite and gives it a local habitation and a name. And he does this not by his intellect alone (which can function as impersonally as a computer), but by everything he is, the heights and depths of his feelings, and not least by his sensuous experience. The artist puts body, mind, and heart into his work of creation. And in what he thus creates from the fullness of his own unique personal identity we see the limitations of time and space made into the medium of what is eternal and without measure, infinity captured in the finite, the spiritual in the material, or (to use technically Christian language) we see the Word made flesh.

What, therefore, we are celebrating in this festival is the marriage of heaven and earth. Heaven is perceived not as some remote, unattainable, perhaps even illusory, state of being, but as present in the works we hear and see, dancing in our midst, a Reality too real to be gainsaid, and most human when most sublime.

It is this inexpressibly rich Reality, made known to us through man and matter, that we have come here this morning to worship. It is the Reality which lies always around us and ever encompasses us, but which we often fail to see because our eyes are blinded as if by scales. But when the artist shares his vision with us the scales fall from our eyes and we see Reality, its exuberance, its majesty, and its homeliness, and we know that it belongs to all times and all places. For heaven and earth are for ever full of the glory of the Lord.

Being a Christian means both recognizing and accepting the fact that all the time we are being created by a power which is other than ourselves but in which we live and move and have our being. In more traditional language it is recognizing and accepting the fact that we are being saved. But since Christian orthodoxy has always insisted that the Saviour and the Creator are one and the same God, or (Trinity Sunday perhaps demanding the language of the Nicene Creed) that the only begotten Son is of one substance with the Father, or more simply, that Christ both created and redeemed us – in view of this fundamental affirmation, perhaps little purpose is served in drawing much distinction between our being created and our being saved. That at least is the witness of the earliest of the church fathers, St Irenaeus, when he said that God's eternal purpose in creating man was finally fulfilled when Christ rose from the dead.

But all that theological talk is potted experience, and can mean nothing until we make it three dimensional, until, in some way or other, it ceases to be theory or doctrine and becomes something we live through. How then do we live through the experience of being created by a power which is other than ourselves but in which we live and move and have our being?

We can't live through it in awareness without reflection, without . . . the prayer of listening in expectant quietness, without contemplation of some sort or other. One of my favourite cartoons appeared years ago in *The Tatler*. It showed two girls emerging from a night club, one of them saying — "What a funny smell"; the other answering — "Yes, can it be the fresh air?" It is by the prayer of listening in quietness that we breathe our true native air which is God in whom we live and have our being, however peculiar that air may first seem to us. It is by this quietness in God that we recognize his creative hands transforming the chance play of events into that which accomplishes his purpose.

For God uses everything which happens to us to create us, the nice things as well as the nasty, that which makes us happy as well as that which makes us sad — when you do well in your Tripos, when Betty agrees to marry you, when you get the right job, when you make good and lasting friends, when you enjoy a marvellous holiday, when your efforts are crowned with success. From one point of view those are chance random events due to a countless series of historical accidents — that your father, for instance, happened to meet your mother. But they are more than good luck of this kind. For God is using them to make you what he wants you to be — a perfectly fulfilled and therefore absolutely happy person. But God can and does use what we call bad luck as well as good, even the worst and most terrible things. In the smoke-filled atmosphere of our unreflective lives, pain seems quite meaningless, just what kicks and tortures us without rhyme or reason. Why should somebody we love be suffering from an incurable disease? Why do we have to endure long periods of irresistible depression? Why do chances mock and changes fill the cup of alteration with divers liquors? The answer is once again the countless series of historical accidents going back to the dawn of time. A valid answer, but not the final answer. For if God was able to put the agony and death of his Son to purposes of infinite good, cannot he do the same with what wounds us? In the prayer of listening in quietness we recognize what God is doing by means of everything which hurts us. As an Abbot of Downside wrote to a friend – ''You are the block, God is the sculptor. You cannot know what he is hitting you for, and you never will in this life.'' But it is enough to know that it is God who has taken over the hitting.

But if being a Christian means recognizing and accepting the fact that all the time we are being created, it also means accepting the complementary fact that God calls us to share with him in the work of creation. The New Testament speaks of us Christian people as the Body of Christ, emphasizing thereby that Christ is present and energizes in us his members. If all the time Christ is creating mankind, it is by means of us his creatures that his creative work proceeds. That is obvious at the most basic level. For men and women have to be conceived, born, nurtured and educated, and this cannot be done without human people to do it. Or to take another obvious but very important example, we have to live in societies which in these days means societies of nation-states. How a nation is governed, its political and legal institutions, the machinery devised for the exercise and control of power – these are fundamental aspects of our environment and, for good or ill, it is to our environment that we owe a great deal of what we are. When, therefore, we study the nature and history of our political and legal institutions, we are discovering one way in which Christ is creating us.

Those great men in the past and present to whom we owe the order and freedom which we now enjoy, it is by means of what they did and do that the creative power of Christ is, in part at least, brought to bear upon us. And when, in our turn, we serve the community by doing the work for which our talents most suit us, the contribution we make to our communal environment is nothing less than Christ in us creating his world. For there is no such thing as a secular job. Either in and with Christ we are helping to create mankind, or we are helping to destroy it. He that is not against me, said Jesus, is on my side. In all worthwhile enterprises, however secular they are generally considered, we can be aware of responding to God's call to share with him in the work of creation.

But we are capable of two kinds of work, two kinds of activity. The first could be called public because it is recognizable by observers outside. We can be seen to be good family men or to be doing something valuable for the community. It is in terms of this public work that a man's usefulness to society is generally assessed. He is a good doctor, or architect, or a good statesman or ballet-dancer or what you will. But important though this public work is – the *sine qua non* of all civilized life in society – it is not the most important work of all. For that most important work of all is utterly private, and takes place in the unseen unobservable life of the heart and will. It is not an alternative to public work, but its pre-condition. And the influence of this private unobservable work is infinitely greater than that of any work which can be seen.

Suppose that on Good Friday evening a sincere admirer of Jesus had sat down to write his obituary. The most he could have told was a story of magnificent and heroic failure, of final ineffectiveness – as the two disciples said to their unknown companion on the road to Emmaus – "We had been hoping that he was the man to liberate

Israel.'' But behind what Jesus could be seen to do and heard to say, behind the public spectacle of what happened to him, there was his inner life completely open to God, whatever the cost, and his heart on fire with love for mankind. That was his private unseen work, the highest form of his activity as man. And, whatever else his resurrection means, it means the assertion that his private unseen work was the most important of all, that it was by this work that he achieved and conquered finally and for ever.

Being a Christian means sharing not only in Christ's public work, but much more in what he did in the inner sanctuary of his heart. It is by this inner openness to God, whatever the cost, it is by this above all that Christ is present and energizes to create mankind. As with Christ, so with ourselves in Christ, the most real work we ever do is that which we do secretly and alone; but we are not alone, for in Christ we are in touch, we are in active communion, with everything that is.

See also 'Death and Resurrection', pages 138—45.

Out of the deep . . .

The mystery of evil – Jesus in his death and passion
overcame evil by accepting it: his experience and
ours – suffering with understanding – suffering
accepted becomes creative – our acceptance of the
evil within ourselves benefits the community – the
fear of death – ready for life and for death – all is given.

Evil by its nature is mysterious as well as terrible. Mysterious, because, although evil is destructive and death-dealing, it must often provide the terrifying depths which men need to be creative. That is the agony, both as pain and the Greek *agon*, struggle, the crucifixion, which people of the deepest vision have to endure in order to find life and to give it. "If my devils are to leave me, I am afraid my angels will take flight as well", as Rilke wrote to a friend in 1907. And most of us will know of William Blake's verdict that "every poet is of the devil's party". In the death-dealing quality of evil there is something without which, it seems, we cannot have an absolute fullness of life. It is the truth by which Milton betrayed himself in *Paradise Lost*, where, notoriously, Satan is the real hero.

. . . In the mystery of evil we are up against one of those fundamental antinomies which we can only accept and can never explain. I mean that goodness can often in some sense require evil to give it wings, so that here we have a hint that the contrast between good and evil is not so absolute as we generally think. If we are to be really alive, I think we have to receive this ambiguity of good and evil. But we cannot receive it without stress of soul and severe inner conflict. I am not talking about the socially inevitable fact that we can seldom choose to do the ideal thing, our circumstances allowing us to choose only between two evils. That brings its own tensions, but they are more superficial. I am referring to the fundamental part which evil seems inescapably to play in the production of good – a terrifying fact from which much conventional Christian thinking hides by separating off redemption from creation as though the Redeemer were not himself the Creator. That separation is a funk-hole which produces either deadness or that protest against deadness which is neurosis. Yet, as a matter of

formal theology and inherited belief, we do admit that evil
is the instrument by means of which goodness is supremely
revealed and supremely effective. Judas Iscariot betrays
Jesus, but the Son of Man goes thereby to his destiny as it is
written of him. And for St John the judicial murder of
Jesus is his exaltation. The men who crucify Jesus provide
the context by means of which he accomplishes his work
and is glorified. But familiarity with these ideas has bred in
us, not indeed contempt, but a kind of reverential insensi-
bility not unlike the sleepiness of the disciples in Gethsemane and on the Mount of Transfiguration.

It has been said that both good and evil are slain on the
altar of beauty. And it is indeed the artist who gives us the
most illuminating hint of how goodness and evil are ultimately one. Dante's *Inferno*, for instance, not in fact the
hell he purports to describe. As a work of art it is a masterpiece of majestic grandeur. Goya's *Witches' Sabbath* sets
out to portray what has been fully accepted as hideous and
repulsive, but it reveals some compelling treasure in that
loathsome scene. Great works of art hint to us that Satan
and Sanctus are one. But until we arrive at that vision in its
fullness we shall remain in conflict upon our life-giving
cross.

Jesus never spoke plainly either about the nature of evil
nor of how he was to overcome it. Most of his talk was in
parables. The parables were not abstract truth, dressed in
stories as though for children, a sort of education without
tears. They were allusive, mysterious, indirect, hinting at
what could not be said. Powerful examples of writing
between the lines, like all great poetry. Thus did Jesus talk.
What did he do?

He accepted evil. He accepted it not of course because

he did not care, nor with passive resignation, a shrug of the shoulder. He accepted evil as his active vocation, as what he had been sent into the world to do. The crowds understood neither his parables nor his acts of healing, and he went his way. "He did not strive", St Matthew tells us, "nor cause his voice to be raised in the streets", unlike some modern evangelists. When the leaders of the church plotted his downfall, he walked quietly into their trap. Surrounded by eleven friends, some of them armed, he did not try to stop Judas leaving the upper room. He gave himself up to the soldiers who came to arrest him. He said little to the church leaders when before them on trial; he did not protest to the soldiers who guyed him; he did not try to make Pilate do his duty; he did not answer the jeers of the mob, and when afterwards his disciples looked for words to describe him, they chose from the Old Testament a verse which ran, "He was led as a lamb to the slaughter, and as a sheep before her shearers is dumb, so opened he not his mouth."

All this, however, was external evil – what others did to Jesus. What of himself? His thoughts? Brave men have gone to deaths at least as painful as crucifixion, heretics for instance at the stake, sometimes with gladness and peace and often without signs of agony and bloody sweat. Doubtless the natural fear of physical pain was present to Jesus in Gethsemane, but his agony suggests an experience infinitely more destructive, an experience of evil and of evil within his own heart. We can only imagine its contents. Hatred at love rejected? Desire to revenge himself upon his persecutors? Rage at the God who had led him where he was? Savage, cynical disillusion? Despair, now at long last he was cruelly alone? A total collapse of faith in anything? "We may not know, we cannot tell, what pains he had to bear."

But the most desolating pain is the pain within the

soul, when all is dark except the emptiness we see, and all is
silent except the noise of passions ringing us for dead. And
what was Jesus doing in Gethsemane but accepting all this
within himself as part and parcel of what he was? For when
we talk of the evil within a man, the word "within" is meta-
phorical. Strictly speaking, the evil is not within a man, it is
the man. And whatever the evil Jesus discovered as he knelt
alone in Gethsemane – whether hatred, anger, malice,
despair – that evil he discovered as himself, as his own
heart. He did not contemplate the cup of which he spoke;
he drank it like a poisoned chalice. And the drinking of the
bitter draught brought no alleviation, for as some hours
later he was dying on the cross, the last words on his lips
were, "My God, my God, why has thou forsaken me?"
Dark, unfeeling and unloving powers determine human
destiny. What further need have we of witness to the truth
of those words, we who believe Jesus to have been the
supreme example of what a man should be? Indeed, denial
of those words is one of the fundamental betrayals of the
Christian gospel, for their truth is imprinted upon Christ's
passion, like the red colour on a poppy. To be true to our
Christian calling, we must not shrink from them.

> *Our only health is the disease*
> *If we obey the dying nurse*
> *Whose constant care is not to please*
> *But to remind of our, and Adam's curse,*
> *And that, to be restored, our sickness must grow worse.*

T. S. Eliot here talks of disease and sickness. That is truth.
But he also talks of health and being restored, for the truth
is not necessarily the whole truth. If the Christian gospel
speaks of unfeeling and unloving powers whose final

triumph is death, it speaks also of life, of life through and by means of death, life glowing from a love which feels and suffers and conquers. But now our talk is in danger of going over the border into that territory of glib religious clichés, words, words, words, sickeningly like the easy speeches which comfort cruel men.

What use is it to tell a man in absolute despair, that if Christ died he was also raised from the dead, and that we can know the power of his resurrection only if we are willing to accept the fellowship of his sufferings? Those words overflowed with meaning when St Paul first wrote them. By now they have been drained dry even of vinegar, reduced to well-meaning but meaningless chatter, words with which to fiddle while the world burns. The wine remains ever new, the bottles grow old and perish, but the wine cannot be given except in some sort of container.

Our task, and it is one we have not fulfilled, and we will not for the next few years, is to discover how we can substitute contemporary plastic for the animal skins once used. And that is not only an intellectual challenge, a call to re-think. It is a challenge to everything we are. A call to feel more deeply even if it hurts and frightens us, a call to plumb the depths of our experience whether in pain or in joy, for it is only out of the abundance of the heart that the mouth can speak, however intelligent we may be.

I have spoken of Jesus accepting evil. Evil thus accepted by Jesus is recognized by his disciples as the revelation of supreme good. The great tapestry behind the altar in this cathedral* is not a different picture from the ordinary crucifix. Tapestry and crucifix are both one and the same picture. The suffering of Christ is his glory, as St John tells us in every line of his gospel. Christ crucified *is* the power and wisdom of God as St Paul says. But how? How can

* Coventry.

these things be? I myself discovered a chink of light here in a picture by Goya in Madrid. It is called *The Witches' Sabbath*. As its name suggests it is horrifyingly hideous and repulsive. Goya has fully accepted the horror and the repulsion. They are there in every stroke of the brush. But something else is there too. The picture also reveals some compelling treasure, some value so overwhelming that you do not want to rush on to the next room. You want to stay and contemplate some grandeur, seen and communicated by the painter in what he knows is utterly revolting. He can see what we see, but his genius can also see beyond, to where ugliness is revealed as beauty.

Is not the same true of the great dramatists of the world? To playwrights of less than genius the sordid is seen only as sordid, the sadistic as no more than sadism. It is that I think which gives truth to adverse criticism of kitchen sink drama and the theatre of cruelty. But with a Sophocles, a Shakespeare, a Racine and Ibsen, the vision penetrates further. They see what we see of the sordid and the cruel and portray it with terrifying power. But in these things they see beyond to a majesty at which we have not guessed: Oedipus tearing out his eyes because he cannot bear to see reality; Lear driven to madness because he can take ro more of human suffering; Phédre consumed and destroyed by her insatiable passion; the master builder falling to his death from the steeple which he had been persuaded to climb by the young girl who gave him new life. These dramas harrow and terrify us, almost beyond endurance, but they do not degrade. They are not in the least bit sick. Quite the contrary. They uplift. They uplift because they enable us to see more deeply than before, showing us unspeakable riches in the very people whose bankruptcy they have fearlessly portrayed.

True art, visual or dramatic, is prophecy. It speaks about ourselves and shows us what we are, as did supremely the drama of Christ's death and passion. Can we discover the treasure hidden in the rubbish dump, hidden in the reeking rubbish dumps which litter some areas at least of our own lives? For that is where the treasure lies – in our own Gethsemanes and Calvaries even more than when we contemplate the lilies of the field how they grow. . . .

But if we are to find the hidden treasure, there is one thing we must at all costs avoid. We must *not* delude ourselves into thanking God that we are not as other men, not like Oedipus, not like Lear, not like the men who robbed the bank, not like the woman who murdered her mother. In Gethsemane, Jesus discovered and accepted that he was these people and a disciple must not imagine that he is greater than his master. We must recognize, like Jesus, that we are of the same stuff as the people we tend to pity or condemn. We cannot know ourselves as the Christ displayed in the Sutherland Tapestry, unless at the same time we recognize ourselves as kneeling with him in the Gethsemane Chapel, finding in our own hearts the evil acted out around us. Cover the rubbish dumps of your life with undertaker's grass, manufacture some spiritual airwick to dull your nose to its stench, and you cut yourself off from all possibility of finding the glory which Christ has shown to be there.

What, then, to return to a concrete individual, what can we do for the man who comes to us in absolute despair? If we have not hidden away from ourselves, we shall be less likely to sidestep his agony. When we are embarrassed, or tongue-tied or speak of other things, it means that we are frightened. Frightened because the man's fully articulated despair threatens to remind us of our own despair, so far successfully evaded. So we stutter in what we think is our desire to help or talk about last week's football match, in order, as we think, to take the man's mind off himself, when in fact it is ourselves we are protecting, not him. To the degree, however, in which we have faced and accepted what is within us, what we are, to that degree the man will not frighten us. If there is silence it will not be unnatural and if the man talks and talks and talks and talks about the hell he is in, we shall be ready to listen without nervous interruption, because we ourselves have also entered those deserts of despair, and found them a place where living waters flow. But to tell him that would be a cruel mockery, for he must first accept the arid desert and only he himself can do that. Only he himself by accepting the arid desert can discover the living waters and his endless talking shows him to be on the road to acceptance, though he does not know it. Offer him whisky if you like but do not offer him the salt water of spiritual consolation.

Two days after Jesus died a woman was weeping near his tomb. The figure who approached her did not try to stifle her grief, he tried to elicit it. "Woman," he said, "why weepest thou? Whom seekest thou?" She spoke of what was in her heart, disclosing what at that moment she most truly and fully was. People identify what they are with the names they bear. For me my name summarizes what I am. So the figure spoke her name. He said unto her "Mary" and at that moment her sorrow was turned into joy. Yet she had made no mistake. Jesus had truly died. She was told not to cling to him and clutch him, as though he had not.

But is the acceptance of sorrow the same as the acceptance of sin? Suppose I have murdered somebody to steal his money. Must I accept that too? Indeed, yes. Only if

I can accept myself as the sort of person who did the murder, only if I can accept as my own the rational guilt for that terrible deed, only after that agony and bloody sweat, can I discover new life and peace. That is the reality which lies behind the tradition of our confessing our sins. Not to win concessions from a potentate; not to gain his approval and get once more on the right side of him, but to receive what we are. The factors of heredity and environment which have helped most powerfully to make us what we are, must not be ignored. For what I have to receive is not a hypothetical me, a me whose father was not a drunkard, and whose mother was not a tart, but the actual me as I am. I must, in other words, receive both that for which I am responsible and that for which I am not, and how in any case can I discriminate accurately between the two?

Dons and priests are like the attendants at a left luggage office, they want to label everything. They behave as though a thing is not a thing unless it has a label. Let us therefore accept this compulsive infirmity, and give a label to what has been said. Let us stick on it a piece of paper on which are printed the words Creative Freedom. The Christian answer to the fact of evil is the fact of our creative freedom. From one point of view we are the slaves of circumstance, from another we are free men, because by accepting our slavery, we can use it to express our freedom. What else is meant by the Christian affirmation that Christ reigns from the cross? Circumstances held him in their iron grip and he did not ask for an impossible release from them, begging his friends, shall we say, or his God, to take out the nails. But by accepting them, he made them say what he wanted to say and he made them do what he wanted to do. For he wanted to speak of the power of love to conquer circumstances, and neither his teaching nor his words of mercy had got that truth over, even to his chosen disciples. But what activity in words and works had failed to do, acceptance of circumstance achieved. "I, if I be lifted up, will draw all men unto me". Receiving his sufferings, he made them reveal to millions down the ages the unconquerable strength of self-giving love. His slavery thus became a medium of his supreme freedom, the iron grip of circumstance the instrument of creation.

Freedom and creativity go together. It is because he has found freedom in necessity that the sculptor creates beauty from solid blocks of marble. It is because he has found freedom in necessity that the poet reveals truth in the rhyme and rhythm of words, which remain their clumsy and intractable selves. It is because he finds freedom in necessity, that the scientist opens to us doors to knowledge hitherto locked, by accepting the brute facts of his laboratory experiments. So, also, when a wife is unfaithful, a child dies, a business collapses, or when we become aware of the nasty or horrifying qualities of our own temperament, we can accept and receive the real and terrible agony of it, and thus finding our freedom we are able to create goodness and love.

When at the end of the last century, Lord Frederick Cavendish was assassinated in Phoenix Park, his widow took special care to convey to the assassins her concern for them. In that tragedy she found her freedom and created goodness. A man deprived of wife and family for this reason or that, can use his experience of loneliness to understand and feel with all who find themselves in a hell of isolation, thus creating comfort and joy. That is the answer to suffering and evil, to make it by acceptance, the vehicle of our creative freedom.

God loves us supremely and cares for each of us intimately. "Fear ye not therefore, ye are of more value than many sparrows." But this does not mean that he will wave a magic wand to protect us from misfortune or to deliver us from human bondage. Life will take its toll of us, and ever and anon there will be darkness upon the face of the deep. But if we will, Christ can open our eyes – we who were born blind – can open our eyes to perceive the darkness as light, to see necessity as the means whereby we can obtain our freedom, so that we shall say, "We should never have known what love really is, we should never have known what living really is, but for the limitations and contradictions of our human lot, the perplexities and the pain." That is what Christ does for us, although he does it in unlikely and unimagined ways. He has already begun to do it – for "God, who commanded the light to shine out of darkness, hath shined in our hearts, to give the light of the knowledge of the glory of God in the face of Jesus Christ."

The superficial answer to suffering is the attempt to escape from it as much and as best we can, to ignore it as far as possible, distracted from distraction by distraction. So we overwork or pursue pleasure relentlessly, clutching at either of them like a drowning man clutching at a straw. Or we tense ourselves up in some way or other, building around us a brick wall whose primary purpose is to protect us from ourselves but which also inevitably cuts us off from others. But this attempt to escape from suffering by distraction or isolation does not work. The power of suffering as death-dealing is not so easily evaded. We may to some extent be able from time to time to forget what is gnawing at us, but the gnawing continues, the destructive force goes on slowly killing us. Our identity is diminished, however successfully we may make ourselves unconscious of the fact for shorter or longer periods. And our oblivion is a double one. For in attempting to escape our destructive suffering we have also made ourselves blind to its potentially creative power. We have run away from our fate instead of becoming its master.

In the biblical legend Jacob wrestles all night with the mysterious stranger who has attacked him and is bent on killing him. At dawn the stranger tries to leave. And Jacob says – "I will not let thee go unless thou bless me." So the potential destroyer blesses Jacob and promises him rich fulfilment, "for as a prince hast thou power with God and with men, and hast prevailed".

When, instead of struggling with our assailant we try to escape from him and forget our suffering, then no blessing or promise can be given. In protecting ourselves by attempted forgetfulness from our fate we also insulate ourselves against the means of becoming our full selves.

Here we should make clear that among the various forms of suffering – physical disease, accident, catastrophe – the ultimate form is always mental and emotional. For the objective illness or accident or catastrophe accomplishes its deadly work in what we call our state of mind or our feelings. It is as beings who think and feel that we are vulnerable to the onslaughts of suffering. And in mind and feeling we can suffer just as much, and generally far more, when our suffering is linked to no physical illness or external distress. For when linked to something objective or external our suffering seems to make some sort of sense, however bloody that sense may be. But when our suffering comes only from within our own heart and mind with nothing outside to pin it on, then it seems utterly and senselessly malignant. We suffer we know not why. But of whatever kind it is, suffering attacks us in the very centre of our identity. It is myself as a person who is mauled.

But if we do not attempt to run away from our suffering, what then is the alternative?

The alternative is to accept and receive it, to take it on as a part of what we are. For in doing this we discover new and hitherto unknown and unimagined areas of our being. We discover that the self we took as our total self was in fact only a small fraction of what we are, that we have reserves of strength, and insight and courage and heroism and love and compassion of which so far we have been totally unaware. That is how suffering can by acceptance create us – by activating and making accessible to us powers within us which hitherto were dormant and only potential so that we had no inkling of their existence. So when the suffering first comes, ignorant of our dormant potential, we feel simply that we cannot bear it. The suffering, we feel, is too much for us and will destroy us. It seems therefore that we must either resign completely and give way to the destructive power and let the waves drown us, or try to salvage some shreds of identity by means of self-pity or by taking the side of the suffering's assault and thereby obtaining some kind of perverse masochistic satisfaction in our own destruction. But this capitulation to suffering so that it drowns us, or we seek to console ourselves for it by self-pity or masochistic pleasure, this capitulation works itself out in terms of the limited self which is the only self of which so far we are aware. It is that limited self which feels it cannot bear it and must be swept away.

Yet when, by miracle, we accept the suffering, receive it, take it on board, then we find that this limited self is an illusion, that we are infinitely more than we ever imagined, so that we can after all take the suffering and in taking it become fuller, deeper richer people because a dormant potential within us has been roused to activity and life, and we know ourselves to be more than previously we had even a hint of. Thus does the destructive power of suffering become creative and what is death-dealing become life-giving.

But we shall not know that this is going on. There will be nothing like a glorious certainty that we are mastering our fate by assimilating it and by assimilating it growing into fullness. All we shall feel is much pain with spasmodic and very faint glimmers of hope. The faint glimmer of hope will be obscure and undefined. It will be a glimmer of hope for we know not what. Yet for all its being feeble, intermittent, and without content, the hope is the call to us of our own future, indicating that we are not only at an end but also at a beginning. For the hope, weak and unidentified though it is, is a sign that a transformation has begun – the transformation of the death-dealing past into the life-giving future. The hope shows that somewhere within us we are somehow obscurely aware that the suffering we meet and receive will call forth a self capable of digesting it, a self therefore which is greater and fuller than the self at present known to us.

But the price of this transformation and growth is willingness to feel the pain of our suffering, however acute it may be. And the pain will generally seem like one undifferentiated meaningless horror. We shall not be able to distinguish between the pain which belongs to the destruction of the limited self manacled to the past, and the pain which belongs to the birth and creation of a fuller self. (For our birth and creation involve pain – the woman in travail is its inevitable symbol.) But in fact when we receive our suffering and are willing to feel its pain, it is both sorts of pain which are hitting us in the face – the pain of dying and the pain of being born. It hurts when the manacles which chain us to the past are broken. And it hurts when by our experience we are opened up almost forcibly to the future. It seems like one single hurt, leaving us all too agonizingly aware of its destructive power and almost totally unaware of its creative power, save for the faint glimmer of undefined hope.

Yet that hope is like a grain of mustard seed which when it is sown is the least of all the seeds, but grows up into the greatest of all plants so that the fowls of the air lodge under the shadow of it. For that first faint intermittent glimmer of hope is the impact upon us of the Eternal Word calling us into our future, calling us into being, so that we grow and become people who can support others in their distress and give them shade now and again from the fierce heat of their own suffering.

The acceptance of our suffering involves . . . the acceptance of dark destructive forces within the depths of our being – the murderous aggression, the jealousy as cruel as the grave, the malice, and so forth. To become aware of the enemy of mankind within us as part and parcel of what we are involves the acutest pain. By becoming aware of our own evil we can . . . absorb it into the positive constructive side of our nature so that the evil is transformed into good.

This recognition, absorption, and transformation of our own evil has effects far beyond our individual selves. For we are inextricably bound up with one another, and what happens to us individually has its repercussions within the whole group among which we live. When we become aware of our own evil we become aware of an evil at work among the group – destructively at work because in the group it is unrecognized, and being unrecognized it cannot be absorbed. By our recognition of our own evil and our

absorption of it, we are absorbing an evil which is communal. And the extent of our recognition and absorption is
the extent to which we are accomplishing something for the
group as a whole. When, therefore, we feel the terrifying
strength of our own drives to aggression and destruction,
when we are tortured by jealousy and are confronted by the
stark frustration of our malice, and when this leads us to
deadness and despair, although we feel completely shut in
within our own damned selves, we are in fact accomplishing
something of inestimable value for the community as a
whole. For the evil which is at work unbeknown in the community, the evil which is driving the community but of
which the community is unconscious, has come to consciousness in us, and our recognition and absorption of it
helps to liberate the community from the evil spell of which
it is unknowingly the victim. . . .

. . . The figure of Christ in Gethsemane feeling the sin
of the world as his own, and thereby taking it away, is representative of us all. We share in that liberating work of sin-
bearing when at the cost of maybe untold mental suffering
we become aware of the destructive horror and confusion
within us. For the horror and confusion are mankind's.
And when in us some part of them has come into awareness
and been transformed by being integrated constructively
with what we are, then to that extent we have helped
forward the redemption of mankind.

Almost everybody is instinctively afraid of dying. Why? I
don't think it is the fear of punishment. I know that what
we do has moral consequences which may be profoundly
disturbing. But in themselves, these consequences don't
make dying any more frightening than living. After all, our
life now is full of reaping what we have sown. Our past

actions meet us every day. Is then the fear of death the fear of extinction? Certainly it isn't. Have you ever tried to make your flesh creep by imagining you had never been born? You can't do it. If you had never been born, there wouldn't be any you there to mind. Extinction would be exactly identical. There couldn't be anything to worry about if there wasn't anybody to be worried. What, then, makes people afraid of dying? It's the fear of losing control over ourselves. True, our control is never complete. All the time we are being pushed about by circumstances beyond our control. Yet within these limits we still exercise a certain sovereignty. Until the ship founders we are still its masters, however strong the winds or rough the sea. Our hand is still on the wheel. Death means our hand dropping away, our no longer being able to steer. We are abandoned to the elements and they must take us where they will. This is the true terror of death.

But this fear of losing control over ourselves is one which is always with us, at least below the surface. You meet it, for instance, when you go into a house where everything is always exactly in its place. The householder can't rest if a single book is not in its proper position on the right shelf. He is thus trying to cope with the fear of losing control, the fear of death, though he probably doesn't know it. Or consider how people grasp at power. On a big scale a Hitler wants to dominate the world. He says it is the mission of Germany to do so. On a small scale, I want to dominate my children, or my friends. I say it's because I know best. Behind the reasons given lies a strategy of defence. My control over others makes me feel more secure against the threatened loss of all control. It is the fear of death which is forcing me on. Or consider once again how fanatically we often cling to the past, refusing to recognize that it is dead. I'm an old man, but on Christmas morning I still go bathing in the Serpentine. It was once a tremendous thrill. Now it is agonizing and always gives me a cold which will one day turn to pneumonia. I clutch at the thrill even though it isn't there and can't ever be there again. We all do that in some way or other. When they married, John and Mary were ecstatically in love. That was ten years ago. By now, the ecstasy should have been replaced by something else; a close companionship, enriching, creative, satisfying but different. Yet they cling to the ecstasy even though it isn't there, and in the nature of the case can't be there. They blame each other for its absence, and are miserable. In fact their misery is due to their fear of dying – of dying to what they once were. So they cling to a dead past.

We sometimes complain of people that they are behaving childishly. A careful analysis of human behaviour shows that most people are in some particular out of date in their reactions to circumstances. A colleague tells me that my talks are hopelessly bad. This criticism is felt by me as a most terrible disaster. It makes me feel that it's hardly worth going on living. I am thoroughly upset. Why is my reaction to this criticism so extreme? Because in my feelings here I am still a small child. My colleague has turned into a parent upon whom as a small child I depend for everything absolutely. Since this parent has turned against me, I am indeed lost. Hence the strength of my feelings. They arise from my not having yet died to my infancy.

There is something in common between these illustrations. In each case I cling on to whatever it is, because I feel that, if I don't, there will be nothing left. I must therefore clutch at some caricature of order. I must clutch at some unsatisfying sense of power. I must clutch at what I was, even sometimes my very infancy. For if I don't, I shall be annihilated. I shall die.

Jesus spoke quite often about this. He emphasized that death is one of the fundamental facts of human life; so if you had asked him what human life is really about, he would have answered, "It's about dying." And he would have gone on to say, "It's only by being ready to die that you will be able to live." Those, of course, are my words. Listen to his: "Whosoever seeks to gain his life will lose it, but whosoever loses his life will preserve it." "Unless a grain of wheat falls into the earth and dies, it remains alone, but if it dies, it bears much fruit. He who loves his life loses it, and he who hates his life in this world will keep it for eternal life." Jesus saw that all the time men and women are being faced with the challenge of death; and that if they are to grow into full maturity, they must not clutch at this or that aspect of themselves. They must take the risk, the awful risk, of letting it go. They must, in other words, be ready to die daily. For this was the path, the only path, to complete life. What Jesus preached, he also practised. He allowed everything to be stripped away from him, and died naked upon a cross. So he passed through the grave and gate of death to his joyful resurrection. "I am he that liveth and was dead; and behold, I am alive for evermore."

This is the gospel. Christ's resurrection assures us that the loss of which we are so frightened, real though it is, is not final. We surrender, we give up, only in order to receive what is better. So Jesus surrendered his human life. And God gave it back to him, now infinitely more than human. "Whosoever would save his life", said Jesus, "will lose it; and whosoever loses his life for my sake and the gospel's will save it."

We can't make ourselves die. We can leave our books

lying about the room in untidy heaps; we can bite our lips and prevent ourselves bossing other people about; we can give up our bathe on Christmas Day; John can say to himself over and over again, "I'm no longer looking to Mary for the past, but for something else, something new"; and I can behave as though I minded only a little when my colleague tells me how bad my talks are. But what's the use of this outward pantomime when all the time I'm exactly the same inside? After all, the inside, that's the real me. We can't make ourselves die. But Jesus spoke of losing our life "for my sake and the gospel's". It's not a matter of trying but of trusting. Trust God to bring home to you the truth of his Gospel in Christ, so that slowly it sinks to the very depths of your being, and becomes no longer just a message but a real part of you. To the degree in which this happens you will find yourself dying – and living. And when in due course the time comes for you to draw your final breath, you will no longer be frightened. The surrender then required of you will be something of which you already have experience. You will know death as the harbinger of life.

If we are ready for life in the sense of being open to its power and possibilities, then we are also ready for death. If we are aware of resurrection in the present, then we shall not be over-concerned about resurrection in the future. What Jesus said about becoming as little children and taking no thought for the morrow applies with special force to our future in and beyond the grave. We live now from hour to hour, from minute to minute, as those who are ever receiving from the unknown, and that is all we need to know.

Ours can be the confidence of a child living in his

father's house whose needs are supplied as, and only as, they arise. Our faith canno ꞓxist in a vacuum of speculative possibilities. Faith is evoked only by the particular situation in which it is needed. (Hence, for example, the impossibility of answering the question, "Would I be willing to be martyred?") For faith is not a static entity which we have or haven't got or which we have in one degree and not in another. It is always coming into being. It is always being created. It is always being called forth as and when it is needed. When the occasion first arises, we feel as likely as not that our faith is too weak to begin to cope. Then slowly we discover that our faith is matched to our need. And the sign that it is so is seldom any glorious certainty or sense of uplift, but simply the fact that, however much we are wounded and hurt, we are not overwhelmed after all, or perhaps better, being indeed overwhelmed, we still retain that spasmodic glimmer of hope. With regard to all the deaths we have to die, including the final death of the grave, we must always remember that sufficient unto the day is the evil thereof and that as our days are so shall our strength be. If we are like little children we shall not worry about what is going to happen next year or even tomorrow.

It is easy for us to forget that life consists in receiving. Yet when we examine our human experience we find that the essence of life is its givenness. "Every wink of an eye some new grace is born." We are continuously called into being, continuously nourished and nurtured on every level of what we are by the givenness of what we cannot make. Our physical life in its givenness is miracle. Our mental and emotional life is miracle. . . .

The miracle of our being given life beyond the grave is no greater than the miracle of our continually being given life here. Creativity is ever one and the same. It is always the calling into being of what is non-existent; and to those who are created it means for ever receiving what for ever is being given. If in this life we know that we are poor, that we are nothing and have nothing which we are not receiving from the unknown, then it will not seem uniquely strange that life should continue to be given beyond the boundaries of physical death.

At the last is joy

Of the love which is laughter, the ultimate joke and
that party towards which we travel but at which we
have already arrived.

The pilgrim's progress towards the Celestial City is no easy promenade, nor can it be done in some luxury coach of total resignation or complete certainty or perfect knowledge or some absolute dream of a prayer. We have to slog along on foot, and the most taxing thing about the path is neither its roughness nor its steepness but the fact that, as Jesus said, it's so narrow. Indeed it is often a knife-edge . . .

But for all the conflicts and tensions we mustn't forget the Delectable Mountains from which we see the Celestial City, if only from afar. Bunyan's picture of the Delectable Mountains is one of the most marvellous in *Pilgrim's Progress*. In terms of Bunyan's story the Delectable Mountains had to be one stage on the road, a temporary resting-place reached when Christian's journey was already more than half over, and which was left behind when the time came to move on. But in life, wherever else we are, we are always also on the Delectable Mountains from which we can catch a glimpse of the Celestial City, the city which is the object of our quest because we know somewhere, somehow, that it is the place where we most truly belong. And while our glimpse of the city lasts, we are at rest. The necessary conflicts of our life are for the time being resolved. And we experience a foretaste of their final and permanent resolution. . . .

The Delectable Mountains can take as many forms as there are people. Your own particular experience of them will not be exactly identical with that of anybody else, since you are a unique person with a unique destiny. Obviously therefore we must go not for the particular but for the general; each person will have his own unique experience of the Delectable Mountains, but we must go for the experience which is common to us all. Some of us are married, some aren't. Some of us are capable of intellectual satisfactions, some aren't. To some of us music reveals Reality, to others it doesn't. Some of us take to religion like a duck to water, others (I am one of them) find it all but intolerable. I have known people to whom rowing in an eight is a mystical experience. There is no need to labour the point further. What we need is a description of the Delectable Mountains which is common to everybody, whoever they are and whatever their talents, predilections or circumstances. If people catch a glimpse of their conflicts resolved, what is the universal form of that vision?

I suggest that it is laughter.

I mean real laughter at what is seen as inherently funny. What is the test of real laughter? It is the ability to see the funny side of your own situation, the ability to laugh at yourself as well as about other people. Without the ability to laugh at yourself, to find delighted pleasure in the comic aspects of your own character and circumstances, laughter becomes perverted: a superior sneer, a transparent disguise for cynicism and defeat, a defence mechanism to give to others and yourself the impression that you are more at ease and less frightened than in fact you are – committee laughter, cocktail-party laughter, self-consciously Christian laughter: "We may be dead but by God we can be cheerful." A man who laughs at himself, who enjoys the fun of being what he is, does not fall into the perversion of laughter. Mirth, like charity, has to begin at home if it is to be genuine.

In one of Christopher Fry's plays an ageing couple talk of decay and mortality. "Shall we laugh?" asks the man. "For what reason?" asks the woman. "For the reason of laughter," is the reply, "since laughter is surely the surest touch of genius in creation. Would *you* ever have thought of it? That same laughter, madam, is an irrelevancy which almost amounts to revelation."

God, we believe, accepts us, accepts all men, unconditionally, warts and all. Laughter is the purest form of our response to God's acceptance of us. For when I laugh at myself I accept myself and when I laugh at other people in genuine mirth I accept them. Self-acceptance in laughter is the very opposite of self-satisfaction or pride. For in laughter I accept myself not because I'm some sort of super-person, but precisely because I'm not. There is nothing funny about a super-person. There is everything funny about a man who thinks he is. In laughing at my own claims to importance or regard I receive myself in a sort of loving forgiveness which is an echo of God's forgiveness of me. In much conventional contrition there is a selfishness and pride which are scarcely hidden. In our desperate self-concern we blame ourselves for not being the super-persons we think we really are. But in laughter we sit light to ourselves. That is why laughter is the purest form of our response to God. Whether or not the great saints were capable of levitation, I have not the evidence to decide. What I do know is that a characteristic of the great saints is their power of levity. For to sit light to yourself is true humility. Pride cannot rise to levity. As G. K. Chesterton said, pride is the downward drag of all things into an easy solemnity. It would seem that a heavy seriousness is as natural to man as falling. "It was by the force of gravity that Satan fell." Laughter, on the other hand, is a sign of grace.

Nowhere in all literature is this point put more devastatingly or more poignantly than in *King Lear*. From the start Lear takes himself with the utmost seriousness. His pride makes him utterly blind and leads him to actions which drive him to insanity and destruction. If only he could see the joke he would be saved. But he can't. Yet the Fool tries continually to make him see it, and Lear's self-imprisonment in a situation where humour is so totally out of place as to be obscene is one of the most horrific aspects of the play. Lear is in hell because he has made laughter loathesomely inappropriate. His egotistical self-dramatization as the most generous of fathers has led two of his daughters to disown him. And he says to the Fool: "When were you wont to be so full of songs, sirrah?" To which the Fool answers: "I have used it, nuncle, ever since thou madest thy daughters thy mothers": ever since "thou gavest them the rod and put'st down thine own breeches." Or when in madness Lear tears off his clothes, the Fool says: "Prithee, nuncle, be contented; 'tis a naughty night to swim in." If in the intolerable grimness of his self-inflicted torture Lear could have risen to the merest flicker of a laugh, he would have been a man redeemed. The pride which from the first has made him incapable of laughter is the essence of his appalling tragedy.

So, from the bottom of your heart thank God when you can see the joke popping out of your circumstances, even when they are grim. Thank God when you can take a delighted pleasure in the comic spectacle which is yourself, especially if it is yourself devoutly at prayer. (Why am I like a famous jackdaw?) Thank God when you can laugh. It means that you are on the Delectable Mountains and that your redemption has drawn nigh. . . .

If by laughter I accept myself, it is by laughter that I also accept others. Everybody has warts. The only alternatives are to get angry about the warts or to laugh about them. To pretend that they don't exist is to be like the courtier in the fairy story who heard a cow mooing, and thinking it was the Princess, said: "Listen, how beautifully she sings." But laughter is realistic. It is an acceptance of somebody warts and all. "Real laughter is absolutely unaggressive; we cannot wish people we find amusing to be other than they are; we do not desire to change them, far less to hurt or destroy them'' (Auden). It is, for instance, always Mrs Malaprop who gets the loudest applause at the end of the play. In the very absurdity of her idiotic intellectual pretensions she is revealed as lovable somehow. Sheridan's achievement is to give us eyes to recognize the Mrs Malaprops we meet off-stage and in our laughter to love them.

And another very important thing to notice is that in the love which is laughter we never try to get something for ourselves on the sly from the people we think we love. The most common perversion of love is a disguised acquisitiveness, a possessiveness which murders love. But a love which laughs is never possessive or on the make. It is too delighted with the caperings of the other person to have any time to think of itself. ''That is why a man in a passion of any kind cannot be made to laugh. If he laughs, it is a proof that his passion has been dissipated'' (Auden).

Altogether, I suggest that laughter is the best and clearest reflection we ever get in this world of God's love for his creation. In laughter we see the Celestial City in what is more than a passing glimpse.

So far, however, we have been considering laughter only in our personal relations – with ourselves and with others. But laughter has also a metaphysical dimension, by which I mean that it is closely bound up with our most fundamental beliefs and deepest commitments . . . we have to live on several different levels of being at the same time. And the levels inevitably clash with each other. A man may on one level, for instance, have a sturdy independence of character while on another level he may be utterly dependent. I forget of what Roman emperor it was said that he was a great leader of men and follower of women. Another man may have the deepest faith in God's perpetual Providence and be terrified in an aeroplane. There are clever fools and unlearned philosophers. There are hard-headed businessmen who will weep at the death of Mimi each time they see her die. There are men of prayer who are almost suicidal if they miss a train. Such incongruities between the various levels of our existence are the very essence of humour, and when we perceive them we can't help laughing.

The situation is made all the more comic by the fact that each level of our existence is some sort of self-consistent whole. If we keep within the limits of one particular level, then everything fits together neatly – neatly enough, indeed, to be positively dull. But bring in another level of existence, and the clash between the two independent self-consistent levels makes everything go haywire. During the war, for instance, Stalin once asked Churchill how many troops were at the disposal of the Vatican. To which Churchill replied: "Several legions, not all of them visible on parade." The juxtaposition of time and eternity is always laughable. I found the converse of the Churchill story in a Christmas number of the *New Yorker*, there was a drawing of the stable at Bethlehem with the caption, "But we wanted a girl." Necessity and contingency are indeed very odd bedfellows. And that is the whole glory – and the whole joke – of Christian faith. Our experience drives us to believe two completely opposite things at once, and what, in the last resort, can we do but laugh at the sheer ludicrous fun of it all?

In terms of time the eternal Lord of all order appears to be the Lord of misrule. No wonder the pharisees, who seem to have been always wholly serious, had to have Jesus put down. He couldn't be allowed to go on indefinitely standing everything on its head and making their piety look ridiculous. Why, in the end, they might even laugh themselves, and that would be the ultimate catastrophe. Who in reality had ever witnessed a pious man blowing a trumpet before he put a pound note in the church box? The notion was irresponsibly misleading. And then there were camels going through the eyes of needles, not to mention camels being swallowed easily by those who choked when they swallowed a gnat. And if people did sometimes get a speck in their eye who ever heard of a man, and an improving teacher at that, who had a log in his? And worse: idlers who were given full pay, stewards who were successful cheats, spendthrift and debauched sons being fêted on their return home – what had all this pernicious nonsense to do with religion? It could only undermine the morals of society, and, being socially dangerous had to be stopped; stopped before the contagion of eternal love showed up the whole solemn system of moralism and religiosity as a complete knockabout farce. So the Jester had to be crucified.

But Eternity had the last laugh after all. For that is the final joke – the resurrection. Here are Caiaphas and all his crowd, Pilate and Herod and all theirs, sitting complacently in a state of grave and dignified self-congratulation. They have done their duty and justified the authority vested in them by efficiently disposing once for all of a dangerous fool. He is safely dead. And with solemn calm again restored they can concentrate once more on the really serious matters to which their lives are dedicated. But behind their backs, without them having the slightest inkling of what is going on, the fool has popped up again like a Jack-in-the-box and is dancing about even more vigorously than before and even more compellingly. People here, there and everywhere are falling under his spell. But the brass hats and mitred heads and stuffed shirts are facing the other way and can't see what is going on. So they continue with their dignified mutual congratulation and their serious business.

If that isn't funny, nothing is. It is the supreme, the final, the ultimate joke – that than which nothing could be funnier. And since laughter, although not irresistible is none the less highly contagious, perhaps the brass hats themselves will in time catch the disease, turn round, see the joke, and laugh with the rest of creation because the kingdom of God has drawn near.

And the fun continues in heaven which, as Julian of Norwich said, is right merry. Perhaps – who knows? – we shall see Athanasius and Arius laughing together at the absurdity of their theological definitions; or Augustine and Pelagius slapping each other on the back instead of in the face. We may even see Mr Gladstone enormously and unashamedly enjoying the company of those he has mistaken for fallen angels. But the best of it will be those white robes supplied by the celestial Moss Bros, because they certainly won't fit and we shall all look like dustmen got up as dukes. And the fun of that will make the party go with a bang.

On the Delectable Mountains of laughter we sense the glory which shall be revealed in us. Indeed we know the glory is already ours, and that is what makes our present ragamuffin state so deliciously ludicrous. At Mirfield in our Community church we sit in order of seniority. The places occupied by the oldest men are known as Cemetery Row. "I see you've been moved up to Cemetery Row", we say to an elder brother. That Community joke makes the hottest kind of evangelism look by contrast like the negation of God. For through the joke of Cemetery Row there rings the laughter of the universe, and there isn't much laughter in hot gospel unless you see how funny it is.

The incongruity between death and fullness of life gathers up all the other incongruities, all the contradictions, conflicts, and tensions which in this world must be not only accepted but positively welcomed and joyfully received. For it is only when we thus welcome and receive them that we discover, when all is said and done, how laughable they are. And although we are still on our journey, when we laugh we know that really we have already arrived. The party has begun and we are there.

Sources of selected passages

Pages
147   ibid., p. 17.
148   ibid., p. 37.
148–50   ibid., pp. 33–36.
150–54   ibid., pp. 41–47.
154–55   *Tensions*, pp. 78–80.
155–59   *Becoming What I am,* pp. 57-62.
159–62   ibid., pp. 67–71.
162   ibid., p. 63.

             New Values
164   *Theology* (September 1962), p. 504. From a
             letter.
164–65   *True Resurrection,* pp. 116–18.
165   ibid., p. 12.
165–68   *Soundings,* pp. 80–82.
168–73   *Poverty, Chastity and Obedience*, pp. 71–77.
173–76   ibid., pp. 59–63.
176–77   ibid., pp. 58–59.
177–80   ibid., pp. 40–44.
180–82   ibid., pp. 83–86.
182–85   *God's Wisdom in Christ's Cross*, pp. 24–27.

             Belonging
187   *Jesus and the Resurrection*, p. 94.
187–89   *True Resurrection*, pp. 123–25.
189–90   *The Joy of God*, pp. 109–11.
190–91   *The True Wilderness*, pp. 149–50.
191–94   ibid., pp. 100–103.
194–96   *The Joy of God*, pp. 69–71.
196–98   *More Sermons from Great St Mary's*, pp.
             91–93.

Pages

joining the Community of the Resurrection, Mirfield.

Out of the deep . . .

228–29   *Tensions*, pp. 38–40.
229–37   From 'The suffering of mankind', a lecture given in Coventry Cathedral on 5 December 1966.
237–38   *The True Wilderness*, pp. 97–98.
238–42   *True Resurrection*, pp. 152–55.
242–43   ibid., pp. 165–67.
243–47   *The Four Last Things* (A. R. Mowbray and Co. Ltd, 1960), pp. 7–11.
247–48   *True Resurrection*, pp. 180–81.
248–49   ibid., pp. 176–77.

At the last is joy

251–59   *Tensions,* pp. 108-20.

Books by H. A. Williams

Jesus and the Resurrection (Longmans, Green and Co., 1951)

God's Wisdom in Christ's Cross (A. R. Mowbray and Co. Ltd, 1960)

The Four Last Things (A. R. Mowbray and Co. Ltd, 1960)

The True Wilderness (Constable, 1965)

True Resurrection (Mitchell Beazley, 1972)

Poverty, Chastity and Obedience (Mitchell Beazley, 1975)

Tensions (Mitchell Beazley, 1976)

Becoming What I Am (Darton, Longman and Todd, 1977)

The Joy of God (Mitchell Beazley, 1979)

Some Day I'll Find You (Mitchell Beazley, 1982)

Contributor to:

Good Friday at St Margaret's, edited by Charles Smyth (A. R. Mowbray and Co. Ltd, 1957)

Lenten Counsellors, second series (A. R. Mowbray and Co. Ltd, 1962)

Soundings, edited by A. R. Vidler (Cambridge University Press, 1962)

Objections to Christian Belief (Constable, 1963)

Traditional Virtues Reassessed, edited by A. R. Vidler (SPCK, 1964)

The God I Want, edited by James Mitchell (Constable, 1967)

Sermons from Great St Mary's, edited by Hugh Montefiore (Fontana, 1968)

More Sermons from Great St Mary's, edited by Hugh Montefiore (Hodder and Stoughton, 1971)